Endorsement for *Bible Basic Training*
by Jeff and James Jay

"If you are hungry for training in the Christian life or to be a trainer and if you like grasping a subject through analogy, as I do, you will appreciate *Bible Basic Training*. The brothers Jay have created a very biblical and useable guide to becoming a disciple of Jesus Christ. The text is easy to read and to relate to even if you have never been in the military. The analogy is so compelling that the reader is motivated to apply himself to becoming a mature, effective, follower of Christ. I believe this is one of the best discipleship tools available today."

—**Roger Cotton**
Professor of Old Testament, Assemblies of God
Theological Seminary, Springfield, MO

"If you are going to read one book to find or enrich your spiritual life, then this should be the one. Just like the process that transforms civilians into Soldiers, this manual will give you the basic and advanced biblical skills for your spiritual preparedness and fitness. Read it, live it, and be transformed."

—**Mike Repass**
Jeff's former combat commander

"A solid and beautiful book helping people grow into Christian maturity in the faith and in the knowledge of the Son of God!"

—**Hye Jin Lee**
Pastor, Korean Evangelical Holiness Church

"Even if you are not a veteran, *Bible Basic Training* will help you realize the necessity of being on guard against the enemy, and the dangers of a watered down faith."

—**G. Wiley Gladney**
Pastor of Discipleship
The United Methodist Church of Whitefish Bay, WI

"Jeff and James Jay have hearts directed at helping new believers grow in their faith, and an unwavering conviction that God's Word is the best source for spiritual direction. This book reflects that passion and will help men and women discover biblical truth for life."

—**John Fuller**
Broadcaster

"The world's language disparity makes it difficult to communicate a single message to all. Here the Jay brothers provide a sorely missing, no nonsense Field Manual for the modern military spiritual warrior. Using common operational language we see the heart of what it means for all of us to be fully mission capable soldiers of God."

—**Brad Lewis**
Army Chaplain

BIBLE

BASIC

TRAINING

BIBLE

BASIC

TRAINING

BECOMING A CAREER SOLDIER
IN GOD'S ARMY

JEFF JAY AND
JAMES JAY

WinePressPublishing
Great Books, Defined.

© 2011 by Jeff Jay and James Jay. All rights reserved.
2nd printing in 2012.

© 2011 Artwork by Randy R. Sides.

WinePress Publishing (PO Box 428, Enumclaw, WA 98022) functions only
as book publisher. As such, the ultimate design, content, editorial accuracy,
and views expressed or implied in this work are those of the author.

All scripture quotations, unless otherwise indicated, are taken from the *New
King James Version*®. Copyright © 1982 by Thomas Nelson, Inc. Used by
permission. All rights reserved.

ISBN 13: 978-1-60615-225-6
ISBN 10: 1-60615-225-4
Library of Congress Catalog Card Number: 2010903498

CONTENTS

INTRODUCTION

*B*IBLE BASIC TRAINING is the first book in "the Enlistment Series" that draws parallels between the Christian life and a military career using both Scripture and personal experiences. Enlisting in military service and becoming a believer in Christ are voluntary actions and a personal choice. Military enlistments are for one to six years at a time. The military goes to great lengths to get people to enlist and reenlist. Various incentives help soldiers to reenlist including offers for cash bonuses, college money, choices for where they might live, or the possibility of changing jobs if another is preferred. After weighing all the options, enlisting or reenlisting is often the best financial or career decision. In a similar fashion, many people enlist into the Army of God after determining that life with God is the best choice.

Enlisting in the Army of God, however, is intended to be a lifelong decision. Among many Protestant denominations (evangelicals, born-again, and Bible believing) the moment of decision (becoming a believer) is historically the central sought after experience. New believers are encouraged to become a part of a church family but in many cases discipleship goes largely neglected.

We believe participation in an intentional discipleship process is as vitally important to the spiritual lives of all Christians, just as basic training is critical within the military. Once you have signed up, training always follows the initial commitment. Not showing up for military training at the agreed upon time is a "breach of contract" with the government. This results in dire consequences. Although becoming a Christian requires no contract, we will face potentially dire consequences in life if we neglect our discipleship training. Many times, new believers are not even aware spiritual training is necessary and sometimes suffer hardships as a result. Military and Christian training prepares you to fully function in your new environment. Being aware of the duties, responsibilities, and entitlements gives us the means to contribute significantly to the organization. Christianity is not just about the moment of salvation; it is not an attempt to make us more like everyone else in a group; nor is it getting our ticket punched for our eventual "flight" to heaven and into eternal life with God. It is about becoming more like God today and every day of the rest of our lives. If we continue with our training then a life of peace and joy is our reward.

I can assure you your decision to follow Jesus Christ is not only wise but also life-changing. At the moment of salvation we are God's children and he accepts us as we are but our knowledge of Scripture and our application of truth allow us to experience more of God's blessing. The purpose of *Bible Basic Training* is to introduce us to God's Word (the Bible). We will discuss biblical truths and give you the tools necessary to succeed throughout your spiritual journey. Military basic training has a determined end when you graduate. Both military and spiritual life are intended to be ongoing, lifelong experiences. Let us all continue the process of learning to become "All we are intended to be."

CHAPTER 1

ENLISTING
IN THE ARMY OF GOD

I am the door, if anyone enters by me, he will be saved, and
will go in and out and find pasture. The thief does not come
except to steal, and to kill, and to destroy.
I have come that they may have life and that
they may have it more abundantly.
—John 10:9-10

BECOMING A CHILD of God (a believer) simply requires one
to recognize their need for God. However, following through
to becoming a disciple of God is another story. Scripture clearly
states that salvation comes to those who believe in Christ Jesus
(Rom. 10:9).

The United States military has a formal oath of enlistment all new enlistees go through. After signing on the dotted line the enlistment process also includes repeating an oath. The Army enlistment oath reads:

> I, (state your name), do solemnly swear (or affirm) that I will support and defend the Constitution of the United States against all enemies, foreign and domestic; that I will bear true faith and allegiance to the same; and that I will obey the orders of the President of the United States and the orders of the officers appointed over me, according to law and regulations. So help me God.

Drill sergeants directly influence soldiers. In a similar supervisory role, though not nearly as intimidating, God directs our spiritual lives. Drill sergeants get to know those they train but God already knows exactly who we are. Speaking to the prophet Jeremiah the Lord said, "Before I formed you in the womb I knew you; before you were born I sanctified you" (Jer. 1:5). Jesus told his disciples not to worry because "the very hairs of our head are all numbered" (Lk. 12:7). God knows us and wants us to learn more about him throughout our lives. As his children, I assure you God wants us to succeed.

God loves all of us as individuals. Each salvation story is truly unique. Here are some personal encounters with people and their salvation stories I have been a part of.

While in La Palma, California doing door-to-door evangelism, I met a woman who had just found out that day she had a terminal disease. She was afraid of dying and in her desperation needed to know if God was real. She asked him for a sign to prove he was. She saw my subsequent arrival as God showing himself to be real and accepted Jesus moments later. A few hours later she walked into a church for the first time in her life.

In Riverside, California I met a mother who was struggling to get her housework done. After hearing the gospel message she lined up her eight children and they all received salvation.

In Evanston, Wyoming I met a teenager who had just lost her parents in a car crash the night before. She was desperately searching for answers to life after death and whether or not God was real. After a short conversation while sitting on her lawn she received salvation.

As a young college student I spent four hours in jail in Casper, Wyoming after forgetting to pay a speeding ticket. Not one of my best moments. A jailer noticed my college I.D. (Trinity Bible College) and gave me a ride to my car when I was released. She asked me a number of questions about my beliefs so I shared with her my story and who Jesus is and as we arrived at my car she asked to pray with me to receive Jesus as her savior.

While still in high school I decided to become a marine. The recruiter made many false promises saying, "You can choose your job, duty station, and schools." This all sounded great to me. An additional perk he used to reel me in was the opportunity to go to Wyoming Cowboys football games for free. Wyoming is a Division I football team only a couple of hours from where I live in Nebraska. They have an explosive offense and little defense so the score is usually very high and there is a lot of excitement. Everything was going great. But somewhere along the way I started having doubts; it all seemed too good to be true. A few months later, my recruiter got in trouble for making false promises to enlistees so they allowed me to get out of my contract without any consequences. I later joined the Army infantry.

After enlisting in the Army of God, you may be experiencing a myriad of thoughts and emotions. Fear of the unknown can be pretty scary. You might be thinking about what you are giving up, what others may say, or if you've made the right decision. You may start doubting God like I did my recruiter. Recruiters and people in general may stretch the truth to manipulate a response. There is a big difference in our spiritual lives, though. God does not function the way people do; what he says he will always do. The book of Numbers says, "God is not a man that he should lie nor the son of man that he should change his mind. Does he speak and then not act? Does he promise and not fulfill?" (Num. 23:19 NIV).

1. How do I enlist in the Army of God?

If you have not already done so before beginning this study, it is vitally important to make a decision to receive Jesus Christ as your personal Savior. If you have already accepted Christ in the past, this road will be a great reminder of your commitment. By studying the "Roman's road" to salvation, we can develop the theme of humankind's sinful position and God's unmerited love. The "Roman's road" is an allegorical means of explaining the good news of salvation by using verses from the book of Romans. It is a simple yet powerful method of explaining why we need salvation, how God provides salvation, how we can receive it, and what the results of salvation are. Whether or not you have taken this trip before, the "Roman's road" will be a fruitful journey, if you stay on the path.

2. What is sin?

> To him who knows to do good and does not do it, to him it is sin.
>
> —James 4:17

Sin is any action of disobedience to God. It is breaking God's law. A closer look will show you that all sinful activities are harmful to the individual, group, and affect society at large.

A way to visualize sin might be through the eyes of an archer. The archer seeks to hit the target with an arrow. Pulling back on the bow he looks at the target and makes necessary adjustments. The center of the target is the desired place to hit but hitting the center every time is impossible. Releasing the arrow launches it as a projectile toward the target. No matter how much the archer practices he can never be perfect. The archer recognizes when he misses the mark. With this knowledge, he adjusts to improve his next shot. If he does not make an adjustment or he aims just like he did last time, he will either hit the same place on the target or worse with all subsequent shots.

In a like manner, sin is missing the center of the spiritual target. Before believing in Christ all of our efforts to hit the target are in vain. The bullseye is bringing God glory and honor with our lives. Our best efforts without God will always result with errant arrows and life. Even believers are not perfect. The more we practice, though, the closer to the center we can hit. With effort and permitting God to guide our hands and lives, we may even learn to hit the center on a regular basis. Christians are not sinless but we ought to sin less often than we used to as we go.

3. Who has sinned?

> For all have sinned and fallen short of the glory of God.
> —Romans 3:23

Think about who the best person in the world might be. Why do you consider them to be great? In spite of our greatest efforts, we will never be good enough to earn or deserve eternal life. Until we accept Christ as our Savior we cannot please him at all. Everyone sins. We all do things displeasing to God. No one is innocent. Scripture gives us a clear picture of what sin looks like in our lives.

> There is none righteous, no, not one; There is none who understands. There is none who seeks after God. They have all turned aside. They have together become unprofitable. There is none who does good, no, not one. Their throat is an open tomb. With their tongues they have practiced deceit. The poison of asps is under their lips; whose mouth is full of cursing and bitterness. Their feet are swift to shed blood. Destruction and misery are in their ways and the way of peace they have not known. There is no fear of God before their eyes.
> —Romans 3:10-18

Even if our only motive is to act in a way to earn heaven; it will not be enough. Our human agendas behind every good thing we do cause us to work against God rather than for him.

4. What is the penalty of sin?

For the wages of sin is death, but the gift of God is eternal life
in Christ Jesus our Lord.

—Romans 6:23

The consequences and punishment for our sin is death. Not just physical death but eternal death! We all have an appointment with physical death. No matter what we do, our bodies will continue to age and we will eventually die. Spiritual death is an eternal separation from the presence of God, a place referred to in Scripture as hell. I believe those who get into heaven will be unaware of the suffering of those in hell. On the other hand, those who are not admitted into heaven because they did not accept Jesus Christ will be able to see all the glory and splendor of heaven but be unable to enjoy even the smallest morsel of the experience. For all eternity they will be aware how easily this penalty could have been avoided by receiving the free gift of salvation. Their choice to deny God is simply selfish ambition and pride. The "wages of sin" is an eternity of punishment without parole.

Christians believe God is the creator of everything. The first man and woman, Adam and Eve, were enjoying a perfect existence with God and nature in the beginning. God gave them a direct instruction not to eat the forbidden fruit but they ate it anyway. The Devil (our spiritual adversary) told them they would be like gods once they ate the fruit. Christians refer to this act as original sin. Scared and ashamed because of their sin or disobedience Adam and Eve try to cover themselves with fig leaves. Fear and shame now replace the peace and harmony they once enjoyed with God. Killing two innocent animals, God provides a more adequate covering for them. As punishment for their crime God no longer permits humanity to be in his presence.

Both physical and spiritual death are written into the equation. The friends and loved ones we lose have regrettably familiarized us with physical death. Spiritual death is entirely different; it is separation from God, both now and in the future. At the time of physical death we transition to heaven or hell, to glory or judgment. Our eternal destination is determined by what we do. If we do not accept Jesus, then we end up in hell. However, if we accept him in name only, and do not follow him, then he will reject us. As there is a righteous punishment for sin and we are all sinners somebody has to pay the price. God spared us from eternal death (Romans 5:8). Accepting Jesus restores our relationship with God. This is the only way we can gain access to God again. In his mercy, we receive something we do not deserve. Jesus paid for our spiritual freedom by dying on the Cross.

5. If sin is so bad, does God still love sinners?

> But God demonstrates his own love toward us, in that while we were still sinners, Christ died for us.
> —Romans 5:8

God hates sin, but loves sinners. God loved us while we were sinners and under the penalty of death. God sent his Son to die for our sins. Jesus Christ died for us! Jesus' death paid for the price of our sins. Jesus' resurrection proves that God accepted Jesus' death as the payment for our sins.

6. How does God respond when we confess our sins?

> ... if you confess with your mouth Jesus as Lord, and believe in your heart that God raised Him from the dead, you will be saved. For with the heart one believes unto righteousness, and with the mouth confession is made unto salvation.
> —Romans 10:9-10

He forgives our sins and cleanses us from all unrighteousness. Because of Jesus' death on our behalf, all we have to do is believe in him, trusting his death as the payment for our sins and we will be saved!

> ...for everyone who calls on the name of the Lord will be saved.
> —Romans 10:13

Jesus' death rescues us from eternal death. Salvation, the forgiveness of sins, is available to anyone who will trust in Jesus Christ as their Lord and Savior.

> Therefore, since we have been justified through faith, we have peace with God through our Lord Jesus Christ.
> —Romans 5:1

Through Jesus Christ we can have a restored relationship with God. You are able to enter God's presence again.

> Therefore, there is now no condemnation for those who are in Christ Jesus.
> —Romans 8:1

Because of Jesus' death our sins will never lead to our condemnation.

> For I am convinced that neither death nor life, neither angels nor demons, neither the present nor the future, nor any powers, neither height nor depth, nor anything else in all creation, will be able to separate us from the love of God that is in Christ Jesus our Lord.
> —Romans 8:38-39

Here is a simple prayer (similar to the oath of enlistment into the armed forces) that you can pray to God. Saying this prayer is a way to declare to God that you are relying on Jesus Christ for your salvation. The words themselves will not save you. Only faith in Jesus Christ can provide salvation!

> God, I have sinned against you. I know I am deserving of punishment. Jesus took the punishment that I deserve, and through faith in him I am forgiven. With your help, I place my trust in you for salvation. Thank you for your wonderful grace and forgiveness. Thank you for the gift of eternal life! Amen.

Today, or in the near future when you accept Christ, we welcome you to the family of God and into the Lord's Army. Now, do not forget to show up for basic training. Enjoy your enlistment. Our prayer—and Jesus' prayer—is for you to have a blessed new life, one that is more abundant than ever before.

As you begin your enlistment in the Army of God here are some additional encouraging Scriptures.

And it shall come to pass that whoever calls on the name of the Lord shall be saved. In Mount Zion and in Jerusalem there shall be deliverance, as the Lord has said, among the remnant whom the Lord calls.

—Joel 2:32

For by grace you have been saved through faith, and that not of yourselves; it is the gift of God.

—Ephesians 2:8

For the grace of God that brings salvation has appeared to all men, teaching us that, denying ungodliness and worldly lusts, we should live soberly, righteously, and godly in the present age, looking for the blessed hope and glorious appearing of our great God and Savior Jesus Christ, who gave himself for us, that he might redeem us from every lawless deed and purify for himself his own special people, zealous for good works.

—Titus 2:11-14

But when the kindness and the love of God our Savior toward man appeared, not by works of righteousness which we have done, but according to his mercy he saved us, through the washing of regeneration and renewing of the Holy Spirit, whom he poured out on us abundantly through Jesus Christ our Savior, that having been justified by his grace we should become heirs according to the hope of eternal life.

—Titus 3:4-7

Behold, I stand at the door and knock. If anyone hears my voice and opens the door; I will come into him and dine with him, and he with me.

—Revelations 3:20

Take my yoke upon you and learn from me, for I am gentle and lowly in heart, and you will find rest for your souls. For my yoke is easy and my burden is light.

—Matthew 11:29-30

But he who looks into the perfect law of liberty and continues in it, and is not a forgetful hearer but a doer of the word, this one will be blessed in what he does.

—James 1:25

CHAPTER 2

SPIRITUAL CONTRABAND

Behold, happy is the man whom God corrects; therefore, do
not despise the chastening of the Almighty.
—Job 5:17

CHANGING CIVILIANS INTO soldiers is not an easy task.
People arrive at training with an assortment of good and bad
experiences and habits. To purge the individuals of the bad, strict
rules against possessing contraband are immediately instituted. In
military terms, contraband is anything that you are not supposed

to have such as alcohol, tobacco, and weapons. The consequences of violating the rules are severe.

During my basic training experience someone in my platoon was caught with contraband. Mass punishment ensued. Eating became a hasty event. From the time we sat down, we are only given two minutes to finish eating. No talking. No looking around. "If you can taste your food you are eating too slowly," the drill sergeant said.

Like military contraband, spiritual contraband or sin, can lead to severe consequences. Sin is like missing the center of the target. We may be only a little off, or we may miss entirely. Either way, we can always improve. To continue in sin can lead to the biggest consequence of all—eternal separation from God. Our spirits were made to fellowship with God. I cannot imagine what it will be like if God denies us what we desire more than anything else for eternity. There is hope, though. Regardless of what spiritual contraband we may possess, or what kind of sins we commit, God will forgive us if we "confess our sins, he is faithful to forgive us our sins and purify us from all unrighteousness" (1 John 1:9).

God knows we are not perfect but chooses to work with us in spite of our weaknesses. God is a gentleman. He will not force us to change, but his plan for us is to purge our sins past and present. Our spiritual cleansing is not a onetime event. Our sinful nature wants to continue dominance over us even after we commit ourselves to Christ. If we want to be more like God we have to get rid of some things. What needs to go or change is discussed later in this chapter. Holding onto the past sin inhibits our spiritual growth.

When I was in basic training, exposure to CS or tear gas was part of the basic training experience. We were taken into a small room filled with gas with nothing except our clothes and a gas mask on. While waiting outside for our turn to go in, we saw how others reacted. They were hacking and gagging and noticeably uncomfortable with fluids coming from their eyes, noses, and mouths. Their faces were bright red as they moaned and screamed.

I looked around for an escape but the drill sergeants were watching from every angle. Avoidance was impossible so I gathered my resolve as my group entered the CS chamber. My exposed areas of skin begin to tingle and burn in reaction to the chemicals. Once inside we were directed to spread out facing the same direction. The company commander came in through the other side without a gas mask, acting as if there was no gas in the room and it wasn't a big deal. *Was this guy for real?* I wondered.

He told us to take off our masks for ten seconds. I did not want to breathe this stuff in; surely I could hold my breath for that long. He counted very slowly. This was a set up and I couldn't hold my breath any longer. I took a deep breath and the gas entered my lungs. I gasped in pain. We were all ready to get out of there but the commander would not let us. I resisted the urge to dash for the door. Several minutes dragged by. My entire body (inside and out) felt like it was on fire. When the drill sergeant finally opened the door, we all ran out of the building. We were sternly instructed not to touch or rub our skin. "It will only make it worse," the drill sergeants said. The soldier next to me ignored the warning and scratched his face. Immediately he screamed out in more pain than before. That was all I needed to see. Resisting an almost uncontrollable urge, I flapped my arms avoiding touching myself anywhere for the several minutes until the gas worked its way out of my pores.

1. What happened to me when I accepted Jesus?

Once Christ is in your life, the sins of the past are forgiven and your name is written in the "Lamb's Book of Life." Christ himself will reference back to the *Book of Life* when he determines at the end of each person's life whether or not to let him or her enter heaven. Scripture says when we accept Jesus Christ as our Savior, we are born again.

> Jesus answered, "Most assuredly, I say to you, unless one is born of water and the Spirit, he cannot enter the kingdom of God. That which is born of the flesh is flesh, and that which is born of the Spirit is spirit. Do not marvel that I said to you; you must be born again. The wind blows where it wishes, and you hear the sound of it, but cannot tell where it comes from and where it goes. So

is everyone who is born of the Spirit." Nicodemus answered and
said to him; "How can these things be?" Jesus answered and said
to him; "Are you the teacher of Israel, and do not know these
things? Most assuredly, I say to you, we speak what we know and
testify what we have seen, and you do not receive our witness. If
I have told you earthly things and you do not believe, how will
you believe if I tell you heavenly things? No one has ascended to
heaven but he who came down from heaven, that is, the Son of
Man who is in heaven. And as Moses lifted up the serpent in the
wilderness, even so must the Son of Man be lifted up, that whoever
believes in him should not perish but have eternal life. For God so
loved the world that he gave his only begotten Son, that whoever
believes in him should not perish but have everlasting life."

—John 3:6-16

Just like entering the military, a new life begins when we accept
Jesus into our lives. Something new happens. Prepare to meet new
people and have new experiences. Who have you met already?
Christians you meet through the training are referred to as battle
buddies. And just like in the military, you should befriend both
the strongest and the weakest links. Leave no one behind. You are
peers now. You will sweat, suffer, succeed, and celebrate with each
other. To develop camaraderie, privacy disappears and everything
becomes shared space. Though you will experience some pain and
misery, you will be united because of the shared suffering.

United we stand; divided we will certainly fall.

2. Is our salvation and eternal destiny then secured? Does the way we live the rest of our lives have any impact upon our eternal lives?

Paul, the author of two thirds of the New Testament, encourages
a disciplined body and mind as necessary components to spiritual
life in God. How are you doing spiritually? No discipline, no
spiritual growth! Once we are on the path to eternal life, we place
our lives and futures in God's hands trusting he will lead, guide,
and direct us.

Do you not know that those who run in a race all run, but one receives the prize? Run in such a way that you may obtain it. And everyone who competes for the prize is temperate in all things. Now they do it to obtain a perishable crown, but we for an imperishable crown. Therefore I run thus: not with uncertainty. Thus I fight: not as one who beats the air. But I discipline my body and bring it into subjection, lest, when I have preached to others, I myself should become disqualified.

—1 Corinthians 9:24-27

By implication Paul sees the importance of maintaining diligence and discipline in our spiritual journey. It is important to God and should be important to us as well. We do not wish to be disqualified in any way or from anything. Spiritual disqualification is possible but highly unlikely. Scripture tells believers not to give themselves over to the acts of the flesh (i.e. habitual sin without repentance) or they will not inherit the kingdom of God. (We will delve deeper into the text from Galatians 5 in chapter 7 "Internalizing the Army Core Values.")

3. How long do I have to enlist for?

Before military training begins a decision is made to enlist or not. I am assuming you are participating in this Bible study because you have already enlisted in the Army of God. This is an important decision and one not to be taken lightly. To enlist is to commit to something; to follow through; to finish what you start. Before you go any further as a Christian, consider what it means to be a believer in Jesus Christ. On the day you join the (Christian) military you see all of the evidence and your decision is clearly the right one. But watch out for buyer's remorse! "I can't believe I joined up," you might say. It is pretty normal to have second thoughts after a big decision. I encourage you to stop, take a deep breath, and reconsider the reasons why you joined God's Army. There is simply no downside to having God on your side. With renewed conviction; make a lifelong commitment to God. Let the transformation begin.

4. Jesus makes me feel better, but I come with so much baggage. Can Jesus help lighten my load?

Jesus is not asking you to do the impossible. In fact, when you enlist in God's Army you soon find your burden is easier to carry. Going through life without forgiveness and without God is like going on a never ending road march with a fifty pound rucksack (backpack). As the miles start adding up, the weight of the pack seems overwhelming. When God enters your life, you still have the weight of the backpack (i.e. the regrets of the past and the traumas of life) and the long journey ahead. But God will help you carry your burdens, and lighten the load you bear. What once was overwhelming and frustrating can become easy and peaceful, if you allow God to help. God does not take away our troubles and difficulties entirely but he gives us peace and strength to confidently deal with life's problems.

Life is like a long journey with weight on our backs through a variety of climates and geography. If we tire, become too comfortable, and decide to settle in one place along the way, we will never reach our destination.

> Come to me, all you who labor and are heavy laden, and I will give you rest. Take my yoke upon you and learn from me, for I am gentle and lowly in heart, and you will find rest for your souls. For my yoke is easy and my burden is light.
> —Matthew 11:29-30

5. Can you tell me a little about why you enlisted?

We all have a story (testimony) about what God did for us and how we became soldiers in the Army of God. Some people were running away from a deep personal issue. Others joined to fight back, or get revenge over some travesty they witnessed, like many Army soldiers did in response to the 9/11 attacks.

Before going any further in this study, take time to reflect upon the love of God and why you have chosen to participate in *Bible Basic Training*. Remember, Jesus calls all of us to be his witnesses.

Witnessing is not an argument or lecture but rather simply sharing the awesome things Jesus continually does in our lives. We are to witness to everyone, whether they are believers or not. I stand amazed each day when I consider the love, power, and grace of our Lord and Savior Jesus Christ. My prayer is for each of you to experience Jesus in a real and personal way.

6. Is it okay for me to enlist in the Army of God and then sit down in the bleachers to watch everyone else go through the training?

I exhort you; do not merely be a spiritual spectator. Our goal is eternal life in heaven. We must travel down the road of life with our eyes firmly fixed on Jesus (see Hebrews 12:2). Each one of us is unique, has immeasurable value, and has something wonderful to contribute to the greater good of Christianity. Stop being a spectator and get on with your training!

Jesus exhorts us to lay up treasures in heaven and not on the earth (Matt. 6:19-20). Put your energy toward doing the will of God and desire to be more like him every day. Don't sit around doing nothing. The Bible tells us there are many rewards for those who seek the kingdom of God first (Matthew 6:33). When the spiritual world around us becomes more real to us than the physical world, we transform into agents of change instead of observers. Expect resistance when you take action to do the will of God. Resistance may even come from people within the church. Regardless of what others do or do not do, it is our responsibility to compare ourselves to God and make our relationship with him our first priority.

You might say, "I am nothing special, certainly not more than the least important part of the body. I am not very important. I am only a number here. I feel invisible. I do not know what my job is (my position or rank in God's Army), or even my purpose." What part of the body would you compare yourself to? Is that part important or insignificant? God made us who we are today. Are you contributing to a healthy Christian body, or breaking the body down through unhealthy living? Like any human body, believers function together as a single body with many different parts, and each individual affects the entire body for good or bad (see Romans 12:12-27).

We are creatures of habit and habits are hard to break. There will be times in your spiritual journey when you will fall flat on your face thinking you did not really change, and wondering if you are any better off than when you first enlisted. This happens to all of us. We all fall short. We all fail. Isn't it great that we serve a God who loves us not for what we do right but for who we truly are? God's grace is amazing. He loves the greatest sinner just as much as the purest saint. Spiritual life is not pain free. Like the great pain your muscles feel when running long distance, spiritual growth is not always going to be comfortable. We need to have endurance and press on through the difficult times. God wants us to serve him regardless of where we are in our lives, whether everything is good or falling apart.

In the military we are assigned jobs and tasks such as communications, infantry, mechanics, police, or engineers. Every job requires different skills and training. In order for the unit to function to its full capacity, everyone has to contribute something. Some units, like Airborne, Rangers, and Special Forces go even further, becoming elite soldiers by receiving very specialized training. These people bring their additional skills to a mission and complete something that others would not be able to without this training. Nevertheless, though specialized, they are still a part of the much bigger military force.

The apostle Paul speaks about "working out our salvation with fear and trembling" (Phil. 2:12). The idea of getting rid of the bad (ungodly activities) and inputting the good (godly) is vitally important.

> A young man cleanses his way by taking heed according to your word. With my whole heart I have sought You; oh, let me not wander from your commandments! Your word I have hidden in my heart, that I might not sin against you.
>
> —Psalm 119:9-11

Therefore do not be ashamed of the testimony of our Lord, nor of me his prisoner, but share with me in the sufferings for the gospel according to the power of God, who has saved us and called us with a holy calling, not according to our works, but according to his own purpose and grace which was given to us in Christ Jesus before time began, but has now been revealed by the appearing of our Savior Jesus Christ, who has abolished death and brought life and immortality to light through the gospel... For this reason I also suffer these things; nevertheless I am not ashamed, for I know whom I have believed and am persuaded that he is able to keep what I have committed to him until that day.

—2 Timothy 1:8-10, 12

For in fact the body is not one member but many. If the foot should say, "Because I am not a hand, I am not of the body," is it therefore not of the body? And if the ear should say, "Because I am not an eye, I am not of the body," is it therefore not of the body? If the whole body were an eye, where would be the hearing? If the whole were hearing, where would be the smelling? But now God has set the members, each one of them, in the body just as he pleased. And if they were all one member, where would the body be? But now indeed there are many members, yet one body. And the eye cannot say to the hand, "I have no need of you"; nor again the head to the feet, "I have no need of you." No, much rather, those members of the body which seem to be weaker are necessary. And those members of the body which we think to be less honorable, on these we bestow greater honor; but our presentable parts have no need. But God composed the body, having given greater honor to that part which lacks it, that there should be no schism in the body, but that the members should have the same care for one another. And if one member suffers, all the members suffer with it; or if one member is honored, all the members rejoice with it.

Now you are the body of Christ, and members individually.

—1 Corinthians 12:14-27

CHAPTER 3

RECEPTION AND INTEGRATION
(MEETING THE COMMANDING GENERAL)

But the Lord said to Samuel… I do not see as man sees; for
man looks at the outward appearance but
the LORD looks at the heart.
—1 Samuel 16:7

AT THE END of our rope or in a moment of despair, when it seems
like no one can help us, God is there. What the preacher says
suddenly makes sense. I just have to get this – Jesus! When given
the opportunity we accept Jesus Christ as our Savior. Now what?

New recruits can volunteer for military service several months before they actually join. Arriving at the reception station, they are given uniforms and haircuts and quickly start looking and acting like soldiers. Life is going to be different from here on. Life as a believer brings changes too. Christianity is built exclusively upon Jesus. Christians are people who choose to let God be their commanding general. We seek approval from the general of our faith. We may be at a similar place today but rather than changing our physical appearance, God focuses on our hearts.

Nothing says unity in basic training like an "onion peel" haircut. Hair today, gone tomorrow, eh? The hair is cut as short as possible. Running your hands across your head feels as smooth as an onion or peach. Military barbers appear to really enjoy giving this style of haircut. The more hair on a soldier's head the more they laugh when they remove it.

I cut my hair short before I arrived to minimize their enjoyment.

Soldiers reform outside. Everybody looks different without hair. I remember one soldier standing out from the rest of us with tattoos covering his head and neck. Even with his unique appearance he was still one of us. The drill sergeants smiled from ear-to-ear at the parade of shiny heads while moving us quickly out of the sun so we did not burn. Our lack of hair brings an instant bond of unity between the newly enlisted.

Thankfully, Christians do not have to get the same haircut or wear the same clothes. Each Christian's physical appearance remains unique for there is no set standard for how a Christian is supposed to look. The surface of a person does not determine who a person is.

In an Old Testament passage, God directs Samuel the prophet to go find and anoint the next king. Samuel narrows his search down to the house of Jesse. All the sons are assembled outside and wait for the prophet's selection. The prophet looks past the oldest, strongest, and most likely, finally settling upon the youngest; insignificant David is God's choice (see 1 Sam. 16).

God accepts all who want to enlist in his Army. He does not accept you based on physical appearance or your ability to succeed;

he accepts you because you have given your heart to him. What an exciting time for all of us when a new member joins our ranks! There is no sweeter prayer than a new believer's prayer.

Though not a military story, I believe the following helps to further illustrate how God initially accepts us exactly where we are and for who we are.

While working at a jail everyone warned me about a particular inmate. He had felony charges, which meant he would probably spend most of his life behind bars. I noticed he was always in conflict with the guards and other inmates. One day he accepted Jesus as his personal Savior. I will never forget hearing him pray. He was sincere but his language would make a sailor blush. I could not help but smile.

There is forgiveness for anyone who comes to the cross no matter the sin. God meets us where we are and will clean us as he sees fit as we go.

At levels high above the training we do, the general is responsible to oversee those who will be conducting our training. Though personal interaction is unlikely, he is very committed to our welfare and future as a soldier. Jesus has become our Savoir, and in military terms he has become our "commanding general." He, too, is very committed to our welfare and future, but (unlike the military general) he is very interested in developing an intimate, personal relationship with us. Like all relationships, it begins with introductions; so let me introduce you to Jesus, the only begotten Son of God and our Risen Savior.

1. What does the "Only begotten Son" mean?

This is an old English phrase, but in essence it means, biological child. God impregnating Mary in a miraculous manner is the beginning of God's plan. God did not do this in a physical sense (as a man would impregnate a woman), but in a supernatural way he implanted a fertilized egg within Mary. This is not an easy concept to absorb. How this happened defies our finite minds. (God creating Adam and Eve is also hard to grasp but he did.)

When she later gives birth; the Son of God entered the world of humankind (see the Gospel accounts of this story in Matthew and Luke chapters 1-2).

2. Can we get to heaven by any religion that does not recognize Jesus?

No. Jesus is the only way to heaven. We must be part of a religion recognizing Jesus Christ as the only Son of God, that he is God in the flesh, and his death on the cross and resurrection is our only way to get to heaven. (Romans 10:9-10)

> Thomas said to him, "Lord, we do not know where you are going, and how can we know the way?" Jesus said to him, "I am the way, the truth, and the life. No one comes to the Father except through me."
>
> —John 14:5-6

3. Why must we come through Jesus to get to heaven?

Jesus came to earth, not to rule over us but to die for us. He gave his life on the cross at Golgotha to pay for our sins and purchase eternal life in heaven for us.

> For God so loved the world that he gave his only begotten Son, that whoever believes in him should not perish but have everlasting life.
>
> —John 3:16

We honor those who sacrifice their lives for our country, our freedom. In a similar fashion, Jesus' sacrifice is for our spiritual freedom.

> If we say that we have no sin, we deceive ourselves and the truth is not in us. If we confess our sins, he is faithful and just to forgive us our sins and to cleanse us from all unrighteousness.

If we say that we have not sinned, we make him a liar and his word is not in us.

—1 John 1:8-10

4. Does God still condemn believers?

No. The Bible is very clear about this.

There is therefore now no condemnation to those who are in Christ Jesus, who do not walk according to the flesh but according to the Spirit.

—Romans 8:1

And we know that all things work together for good to those who love God, to those who are the called according to His purpose.

—Romans 8:28

5. In what ways does God work for us?

Everything God does for the believer is for our own good. This is not candy store religion, though; it is sweet being a Christian but not always easy. When life gets hard, whether because of our mistakes or something beyond our ability to control within our environment, God will not spare us from discipline or suffering, but will give us a way through the trial (1 Cor. 10:13). There is always a reason for what he allows to happen to us. What does not kill us, truly makes us stronger!

What then shall we say to these things? If God is for us, who can be against us? He who did not spare his own son, but delivered him up for us all, how shall he not with him also freely give us all things? Who shall bring a charge against God's elect? It is God who justifies. Who is he who condemns? It is Christ who died, and furthermore is also risen, who is even at the right hand of God, who also makes intercession for us. Who shall separate us from the love of Christ? Shall tribulation, or distress, or persecution, or famine, or nakedness, or peril, or sword?

—Romans 8:31-35

6. Can anything separate us from the love of God?

No. It seems pretty clear in Scripture that the only things separating us from eternal salvation are our own choices. Our adversary (Satan) uses deception to trick us into thinking this free gift is of no value. If God is able to draw us to himself then he is also able to sustain us in the faith.

> He who began a good work in us, shall be faithful to complete it.
> —Philippians 1:6

There may be seasons when we have doubts or we stray from the path but God always walks beside us. He will never leave us or forsake us (Hebrews 13:5)! Whatever the cause, it seems clear the only way to give up the free gift of salvation is to make a conscious choice to give it back to God.

> For I am persuaded that neither death nor life, nor angels nor principalities nor powers, nor things present nor things to come, nor height nor depth, nor any other created thing, shall be able to separate us from the love of God which is in Christ Jesus our Lord.
> —Romans 8:38-39

Be careful with this verse. Studying the context helps us see that our free will can lead us down paths where God does not want us to go. We might even throw away our salvation, ignoring the gift of God. A better understanding of this Scripture would be *nothing outside of ourselves has the power to separate us from God.* God is your General. He has a great plan for your life and the means to keep you safe along the way. Listen to what he tells you. You will not only survive but learn to thrive.

> Be strong and of good courage, do not fear nor be afraid of them; for the Lord your God, he is the one who goes with you. He will not leave you nor forsake you.
> —Deuteronomy 31:6

CHAPTER 4

GROUND ZERO: CULTURE SHOCK

4

Therefore, if anyone is in Christ, he is a new creation;
old things have passed away; behold,
all things have become new.
—2 Corinthians 5:17

NOTHING PREPARED US for the first day of military basic training. We were squeezed onto trucks for transport from reception station to the basic training site. We looked and felt like sardines all jammed in tight with our gear. Though the travel time was only several minutes we were already stiff, anxious, and uncomfortable. By the time the trucks stopped we were definitely ready to get off. The doors flew open and drill sergeants swarmed upon us like killer bees.

Meeting the drill sergeants for the first time was a traumatic experience. We fell out of the trucks like cord wood in every which direction. The ensuing chaos seared into our minds the fear of the unknown. This was not fun but it was necessary in the process of transforming civilians into soldiers. The drill sergeants yelled at us from every side leaving us with no idea what to do or where to go. Pandemonium and fear were tangible enough to see. Some people were so scared they would not or could not move, wrapping themselves up in the corners of the bus. Some wet themselves. The drill sergeants were fiercely intimidating, demanding our complete and immediate obedience. Even the biggest and the toughest among us were shaken by this event. Somehow, we all ended up standing in the right location in spite of the chaos. As our hearts pounded less loudly in our chests we realized we had survived the initial onslaught.

After a long and exhausting day we finally went to bed. Around one hundred soldiers were bunked in an open bay with a nightstand, wall locker, and bed for each soldier. Exhausted, I fall asleep quickly and deeply.

We awoke from our slumber to the sound of shouting and a metal garbage can being kicked down each side of the bay. Some beds were overturned, many of them with soldiers still in them. Windows are opened, and bedding and mattresses were thrown outside. We had to retrieve our goods and put the rooms back together all while on the clock. Get it done five minutes ago. Pandemonium reigned supreme for the next hour or so.

Before we enlist in the Army of God our lives may be just as chaotic as this account. However, unlike the drill sergeants, God does not come to intimidate or cause confusion. He comes to help us restore order to our lives again putting us back together. Christians are in a transformation process, one that takes time from sinner to saint. Though God does not get in our faces like a drill sergeant, he has similar expectations. He expects us to hear what he requires and obey. Living a life of faith is either his way or the highway.

1. Where do I learn about the transformation process?

God's instructions are contained within Scripture. Scripture is to a believer as water is to a private; you will not survive long without it. Applying Scripture to our daily lives is crucial. As we study the Bible our understanding of God and ourselves increases. Our desires turn from our own destruction (caused by following our sinful desires) to eternal life as we walk in God's ways. He sets our feet on the path of righteousness. We join together with other believers as soldiers in God's Army on a fantastic journey through the vast richness of the *Word of God*. We choose to participate in transforming our mind and submit to the Lord's discipline. His ways are so much better than our own best efforts.

The following Scripture passage encourages us to be diligent with our faith. We are to look forward to the future success by preparing in the present.

> If anyone comes to me and does not hate his father and mother, wife and children, brothers and sisters, yes, and his own life also, he cannot be my disciple. And whoever does not bear his cross and come after me cannot be my disciple. For which of you, intending to build a tower, does not sit down first and count the cost, whether he has enough to finish it, lest, after he has laid the foundation, and is not able to finish, all who see it begin to mock him, saying, this man began to build and was not able to finish? Or what king, going to make war against another king, does not sit down first and consider whether he is able with ten thousand to meet him who comes against him with twenty thousand? Or else, while the other is still a great way off, he sends a delegation and asks conditions of peace. So likewise, whoever of you does not forsake all that he has cannot be my disciple.
> —Luke 14:26-33

2. What does Scripture mean by the word "hate" in verse 26?

Hate is more than simply avoiding someone. It means to shun, to disdain, to wish ill will upon another, or to go out of our way to do harm to another. Then why does Scripture tell us to hate our father, mother, brother, sister and even our own lives? Simply put; God wants to have sole possession of the throne of our heart.

3. What or who is elevated above God in our lives?

For God to change us he needs unlimited access to our hearts and lives. God will remove anything that we elevate above him. This can be a very painful experience as God transforms us into his image and likeness. We become his children upon salvation, but we are transformed into his image as we mature in Christ. Our only choice is to submit to his ways. Resistance is futile. I look back at some of my dating relationships. God was a distant second in my life. I elevated my girlfriends above all else. Instead of allowing God to deal with my lack of focus I chose the hard way, which involved painful breakups.

> You shall not make for yourself a carved image—any likeness of anything that is in heaven above, or that is in the earth beneath, or that is in the water under the earth; you shall not bow down to them nor serve them. For I, the Lord your God, am a jealous God, visiting the iniquity of the fathers upon the children to the third and fourth generations of those who hate me but showing mercy to thousands, to those who love me and keep my commandments. You shall not take the name of the Lord your God in vain, for the Lord will not hold him guiltless who takes his name in vain.
> —Deuteronomy 5:8-11

God is not some distant, uncaring Creator who has no desire to know us. In fact, God says before he created the heavens and the earth he knew us (Jer. 1:5). He wants to have an intimate relationship with us. God wants direct communication with us. Anything or anyone who comes between us breaks down our ability to communicate clearly with one another. God must come before all other people or things.

4. What does it mean to bear a cross?

In biblical times, the cross (crucifixion) is a death sentence. To bear our cross is allowing those around us to know we have a new general in our lives. In order to be faithful to our commitment to God, we (figuratively speaking) put to death our former selves and become new creations in Christ. This sounds pretty graphic but it is only to imply how thoroughly different our future is than our past. If we attempt to live and act the same way we used to we will fail. We have a new commander who offers us training, directions, and missions. Like new soldiers, we are to act differently, hang around a new crowd, and make adjustments to our goals and dreams.

We struggle to get away from our past but it is worth the effort when we see what we can become in the future. I believe it is similar to an old Indian proverb a chief told his children one day as they watched a white and gray wolf fight. The smallest little boy put his hand into his father's and asked, "Which one is going to win, papa?" After a short deliberation the father responded, "The one that had fed the most."

> I have been crucified with Christ; it is no longer I who live, but Christ lives in me; and the life which I now live in the flesh I live by faith in the Son of God, who loved me and gave himself for me.
>
> —Galatians 2:20

5. Why is Christ our only foundation with which to build our spiritual life?

The life of faith, our spiritual life, is a journey. The apostle Paul calls life a race; if we plan to finish we need to pace ourselves and keep up our energy. When constructing a building, we must first level the ground and remove any debris before we can pour the foundation. God does the same thing in our lives. He wants to remove the debris before he starts building. God does not wave a magic wand when we commit our lives to him, instantly changing us into saints. It does sound appealing but this only exists in fairy tales. The process begins immediately but God takes his time as he slowly molds us into the image of our Creator. This can be really frustrating because our tendency is to want God to change us in *our* time. He will not do this because God wants us to be dependent on him each day, each moment.

> Therefore, laying aside all malice, all deceit, hypocrisy, envy, and all evil speaking, as newborn babies, desire the pure milk of the word, that you may grow thereby, if indeed you have tasted that the Lord is gracious.
>
> —1 Peter 2:1-3

At our moment of salvation Christ accepts us as we are. He is aware of all of our sins and failures but he sets us free from the guilt, shame, condemnation, and penalty of our past sins. He works to help us remove our debris. Christ becomes our firm, solid foundation. Are you prepared to cooperate with him and begin building your new life in Christ?

I believe it is important to make a distinction between conviction and condemnation. Conviction is from God whose end result will always be drawing us closer to him and making us more whole. Condemnation, however, is from the world and the devil, and pulls us away from God.

> There is now no condemnation for those who are in Christ Jesus.
>
> —Romans 8:1

Condemnation is from Satan (our spiritual adversary) and results in false guilt and shame. Satan paints the bleakest picture possible following our mistakes. He seeks to isolate and imprison us. When we fail, he tells us how bad we are, how we have ruined everything, and that no one can or will forgive us. On the other hand, God wants to help us get beyond our past regrets and failures. Our past sins are like a cancer growing within us, he reminds us of them to remove the growth and live a cancer free life. He offers us hope and the solution to fixing our mistakes and avoiding them in the future.

6. Who is a disciple?

A disciple is a person who recognizes he has more to learn. He becomes a student who brings himself under the tutelage of another, in order to fill an insatiable need to increase knowledge and understanding. In a deliberate and diligent manner, he seeks to put learning into practice, forming new habits and behaviors in order to be aligned with the teacher.

7. What is the reward for becoming a disciple of Jesus?

You can be a Christian and not a disciple. A disciple is striving to be more like one's teacher, Jesus Christ. The word "Christian" means someone who is a child of Christ. A very natural process, as children grow they look more like their parents. By inference, a disciple becomes more like God. When people look at us they should see a resemblance of our heavenly father.

The reward of becoming a disciple is an increased assurance of our eternal destination, a personal peace as we learn to work with the environment and with the people around us, while becoming more and more aware of the Holy Spirit's presence in our lives.

8. Who is the Holy Spirit?

The Holy Spirit is God (Ezek. 37:14; 1 Cor. 2:10). He is an equal part of the trinity; the Godhead three-in-one; Father, Son, and Holy Spirit. Upon salvation he takes up residence within our hearts and comes to live inside us. He speaks to us when we have tough decisions to make. He becomes our conscience, like Jiminy Cricket from the Disney movie *Pinocchio,* and much more.

The Holy Spirit is not the only voice speaking to us. Our adversary plants ideas in our heads, the world around us sends us many messages, and our flesh (our wicked hearts) will also speak to us in ways contrary to the will of God. Jesus is the good shepherd and his sheep know and trust his voice (John 10:27). Listening to the guidance of the Holy Spirit requires us to get away from the busyness of life and find a quiet place for God to speak to us. Once we quiet the other voices, we will be able to listen to the still small voice of the Holy Spirit.

9. What does Jesus mean by living waters?

Humans are eternal beings. Adam and Eve's sin altered life's equation, leaving everyone an appointment with death. In John 4:13, Christ speaks about taking away our eternal death penalty and giving us the means to live life fully on the earth and for eternity afterwards.

"The Beatitudes," one of Jesus' most famous sermons, shows us the paradoxical nature of Christian living. Jesus turns life and human expectation upside down. He helps the people understand God's ways are beyond the control from outside influences. Prayer is an important means through which we access God. We must learn to accept and be thankful for he lives and acts beyond our human capacity to understand.

> And seeing the multitudes, He went up on a mountain, and when He was seated His disciples came to Him. Then He opened His mouth and taught them, saying: "Blessed are the poor in spirit, for theirs is the kingdom of heaven. Blessed are those who mourn, for they shall be comforted. Blessed are the meek, for they shall inherit the earth. Blessed are those who hunger and thirst for righteousness, for they shall be filled. Blessed are the merciful, for they shall obtain mercy. Blessed are the pure in heart, for they shall see God. Blessed are the peacemakers, for they shall be called sons of God. Blessed are those who are persecuted for righteousness' sake, for theirs is the kingdom of heaven. Blessed are you when they revile and persecute you, and say all kinds

of evil against you falsely for My sake. Rejoice and be exceedingly glad, for great is your reward in heaven, for so they persecuted the prophets who were before you."

—Matthew 5:1-12

Scripture gives us understanding to the paradox of life, reminding us of our limited capacity to influence the circumstances and people around us. Our inadequacies turn our hearts toward God for input, guidance, and direction. Too often, we resist reading the instructions or asking for directions, especially men.

The shock factor of basic training breaks down new recruits. After removing previous sources of strength, they begin entrusting themselves fully to their chain of command, the leaders above them and the military organization to which they now belong. In like manner, a Christian must learn to fully trust God, in order to become a mature disciple of Christ.

DIAGNOSTIC SPIRITUAL FITNESS TEST

PANT
PANT

5

For physical training is of some value, but godliness has value
for all things, holding promise for both
the present life and the life to come.
—1 Timothy 4:8

EARLY IN OUR training it helps to diagnose our current physical
fitness (PT). The Army's PT test—consisting of pushups, sit
ups, and a run—is designed to evaluate overall fitness. Seasoned
leaders mark the official results. The Army rewards soldiers who
exceed the standard and assigns remedial PT to those who are

unable to meet minimum expectations. Better fitness equals better job performance.

Measuring our spiritual fitness is important as well. It helps determine where we are today and where we want to be in the future. Our spiritual fitness test is not evaluated by others; it is a personal evaluation, assessing current and future desired spiritual fitness goals. With spiritual and physical fitness we have all the tools we need to succeed. We just have to exercise in order to maintain or get stronger.

My only PT test failure came halfway through basic training. I was standing in line waiting to do the push-up part of our test. The commanding officer instructed us to stand perfectly still, starring at the back of the soldier's head in front of us. We could not look around. He permitted movement only when the person in front of us finished. Well, my nose itched. It was so bad that I had to scratch it quickly, thinking nobody would notice. I waited until the commanding officer's head turned, then scratched. The captain must have had eyes in the back of his head! He spun around before I could drop my hand back into position. He shouted, "Hey you! Why are you scratching your nose at the position of attention?" Before I could respond he said, "Hit your face!" which meant I had to start doing push-ups immediately. He kept pressing me to do more, and by the time I thought I had done over a hundred he said, "Recover." But I had no time to recover because I was up next in line to do the push-up event. I had no recourse; I was set up for failure. After thirty push-ups I could do no more and I dropped to the ground in exhaustion. I failed the test because of an itch.

Our spiritual life as a believer begins the moment we accept Christ as our Savior. We continue one step at a time like any other journey. God gives us the directions for which way to travel and how to get there. On a regular (even daily) basis we hear these directions as we communicate with him. Since God is the source of our faith, his words of encouragement give us strength as we "plug in" to him. He empowers and enables us to live and serve. God will never set us up for failure. If we are listening, he will give us everything we need to succeed.

If we do not spend time with God we become spiritually unfit. Going to church is not enough. The *Word of God* is like food to our souls. If we eat it all the time and do not exercise our faith, we are going to become spiritually fat and out of shape. In this state we will find ourselves incapable of doing things which were previously easy for us. Spiritual fitness consists of three primary events: prayer, Bible reading and study, and service and interacting with brothers and sisters in Christ within our Church community are all components to healthy spiritual growth.

1. Prayer, the first spiritual exercise.

Our spiritual life begins with a prayer as we "...confess with our mouth Jesus as Lord, and believe in our heart that God raised him from the dead, we will be saved. For with the heart one believes unto righteousness, and with the mouth confession is made unto salvation" (Rom. 10:9-10).

This initial prayer is a powerful, life-changing event. It is communicating with God from the very core of our being. The Bible teaches us that communication with God is a frequent activity. Jesus offers us a model of prayer:

> In this manner, therefore, pray: Our Father in heaven, hallowed be your name. Your kingdom come. Your will be done on earth as it is in heaven. Give us this day our daily bread. And forgive us our debts, as we forgive our debtors. And do not lead us into temptation, but deliver us from the evil one. For yours is the kingdom and the power and the glory forever. Amen.
> —Matthew 6:9-13

It is not God's intention for this model of prayer to become the only means of communication. We should use this as an example of the components we can include while praying. Prayer is recognizing that God alone is the one true God. He is the Creator and sustainer of all. He is worthy to receive all glory and honor. His will is accomplished everywhere, at all times. He alone can forgive our sins. He forgives our sins, which are crimes against his authority and will. We are to offer forgiveness to others in a like manner. As he guides us we can endure even the worst temptations. He delivers us from the enemy of our souls. God rules!

God waits for us to include him in our lives. If we ask him, he does not take away the entire weight of what we are carrying but he certainly lightens the load.

> Come to me, all you who labor and are heavy laden, and I will give you rest. Take my yoke upon you and learn from me, for I am gentle and lowly in heart, and you will find rest for your souls. For my yoke is easy and my burden is light.
>
> —Matthew 11:28-30

> …cast all your cares upon Him; for he cares for you.
>
> —1 Peter 5:7

> I will lift up my eyes to the hills, from where my help comes. My help comes from the Lord, who made heaven and earth. He will not allow your foot to be moved; he who keeps you will not slumber. Behold, he who keeps Israel shall neither slumber nor sleep. The Lord is your keeper; the Lord is your shade at your right hand. The sun shall not strike you by day, nor the moon by night. The Lord shall preserve you from all evil; he shall preserve your soul. The Lord shall preserve your going out and your coming in from this time forth and even forevermore.
>
> —Psalm 121:1-8

2. Bible reading and study is our second spiritual exercise.

We read the Bible because it is a compilation of the interpersonal encounters between God and mankind. God's messages are eternal and applicable to all believers throughout the ages. The experiences of all people within Scripture sustained their faith through a multitude of trials and troubles. Today, these words encourage us to continue developing our personal spiritual fitness. During regular Bible reading times we find answers to our questions. This happens far too often to be coincidental. God frequently speaks to us today through the stories and experiences of Bible characters.

> All Scripture is given by inspiration of God, and is profitable for doctrine, for reproof, for correction, for instruction in righteousness, that the man of God may be complete, thoroughly equipped for every good work.
>
> —2 Timothy 3:16-17

We meditate or ponder God's words, seeking to understand exactly what he is saying to us, and what directions to take in life. Our spiritual journey leads us to sanctification, which means to change and grow into the mature person God wants us to become. We press forward to please our commander. We have a goal, a final destination ahead of us; we want to be in the presence of our Master, Savoir, and King forever. God offers us a road map (the Bible), a guide (the Holy Spirit), and companionship (a relationship with Him). Without God we will not reach our spiritual destination!

> ...as his divine power has given to us all things that pertain to life and godliness, through the knowledge of him who called us by glory and virtue, by which have been given to us exceedingly great and precious promises, that through these you may be partakers of the divine nature, having escaped the corruption that is in the world through lust. But also for this very reason, giving all diligence, add to your faith virtue, to virtue knowledge, to knowledge self-control, to self-control perseverance, to perseverance godliness, to godliness brotherly kindness, and to brotherly kindness love. For if these things are yours and abound, you will be neither barren nor unfruitful in the knowledge of our Lord Jesus Christ. For he who lacks these things is shortsighted, even to blindness, and has forgotten that he was cleansed from his old sins. Therefore, brethren, be even more diligent to make your call and election sure, for if you do these things you will never stumble; for so an entrance will be supplied to you abundantly into the everlasting kingdom of our Lord and Savior Jesus Christ.
>
> —2 Peter 1:3-11

3. Cultivating active relationships with other people within a community of believers is the third spiritual exercise.

We encourage interaction with others, and God commands it (Hebrews 10:25)! There is nothing new under the sun. Someone else is going through, or has gone through, what we are going through today. We gain strength in numbers. Where do we go when we feel like everyone and everything is against us? In a general sense, we all have a myriad of people we can turn to who can help us through the challenges of life. That is why God wants us to cultivate relationships with others. Invariably, we have gone through something that enables us to comfort someone else. This is what the body of Christ does for one another—we extend God's comfort (see 2 Cor. 2:3-7).

> Greater love has no one than this; that he lay down his life for his friends.
>
> —John 15:13

No man is an island. Do not try to go through life or faith alone. Seek good counsel especially when facing difficult decisions.

> Where there is no counsel, the people fall; but in the multitude of counselors there is safety.
>
> —Proverbs 11:14

Screen the counsel you receive. Godless people may have a lot of street knowledge but this will not help develop godliness. Does it make sense to get counsel from someone who is failing in their own life? Seek those who can give you both experiential and godly counsel. As in the Scripture passage below, be intentional about including and excluding people from those who give you counsel.

> Blessed is the man who walks not in the counsel of the ungodly, nor stands in the path of sinners, nor sits in the seat of the scornful; but his delight is in the law of the Lord, and in his law

he meditates day and night. He shall be like a tree planted by the rivers of water, that brings forth its fruit in its season, whose leaf also shall not wither; and whatever he does shall prosper. The ungodly are not so, but are like the chaff which the wind drives away. Therefore the ungodly shall not stand in the judgment, nor sinners in the congregation of the righteous. For the Lord knows the way of the righteous, but the way of the ungodly shall perish.

—Psalm 1:1-6

Faith in God is alive and active not cerebral and static. We commit ourselves to him becoming what he wants us to be. Life and training will definitely be difficult at times but God will pull us through.

For bodily exercise profits a little, but godliness is profitable for all things, having promise of the life that now is and of that which is to come. This is a faithful saying and worthy of all acceptance. For to this end we both labor and suffer…, because we trust in the living God, who is the Savior of all men, especially of those who believe… Let no one despise your youth, but be an example to the believers in word, in conduct, in love, in spirit, in faith, in purity. Give your attention to reading, to exhortation, to doctrine. Do not neglect the gift that is in you, which was given to you by prophecy with the laying on of the hands of the eldership. Meditate on these things; give yourself entirely to them, that your progress may be evident to all. Take heed to yourself and to the doctrine. Continue in them, for in doing this you will save both yourself and those who hear you.

—1 Timothy 4:8-16

4. What does it mean to be ineffective or unproductive as a Christian?

We are unproductive when others are not able to see the light of God within us. When we do not reach out to those who are lost, or lift up our brothers and sisters in Christ, our lives are ineffective. We are not representing God. We seldom attend church or when we do are not really getting anything out of it; somehow we think attendance is all we need. An ineffective Christian does these things; he or she does things their own way, stops listening to God, and looks more and more like the world every day instead of being transformed into the image of Christ.

5. What does it mean to "seek the things which are above"?

We make eternal things more important than our daily business. We do not focus on the things of this world, but rather on the things of God. God transforms us into his image when we focus on him.

6. What does it mean to "put to death your members on earth"?

This means putting to death the flesh. The flesh is not our physical bodies. It is the part within us that wars against the will of God, the part that wants to do things our own way, or according to the ways of the world. Our bodies are wonderful. We are the workmanship of God. Our physical body is not the enemy, but we need to cut ties to the person we used to be if we are to represent God. Our bodies are the temple of the Holy Spirit. It is for this very reason that we are to take care of our bodies and be proud of whatever body we were given. If we are to honor God it is important to take care of our bodies. This means not doing anything that would harm our bodies like using tobacco, alcohol, or excess food. Eating too much and being overweight puts a tremendous burden on our bodies.

When the Bible talks about putting to death the flesh it is referring to our carnal nature. This nature is in opposition to God.

> If then you were raised with Christ, seek those things which are above, where Christ is, sitting at the right hand of God. Set your mind on things above, not on things on the earth. For you died and your life is hidden with Christ in God. When Christ who

is our life appears, then you also will appear with Him in glory. Therefore put to death your members which are on the earth.
—Colossians 3:1-5

7. What is the wrath of God?

The wrath of God is for those who are slaves to this world. The wrath of God is directed toward our acting in a way contrary to God's commands and can be executed while we are living and also our life after. Slaves to sin are people who make no effort to resist temptations. They do whatever they want.

8. Is becoming more like God important?

We are new creations in Christ who are being renewed in knowledge according to the image of our creator. If we want to be more like God, we have to decide what we want to grow in our spiritual garden, and what food we are going to eat. We cannot hold onto a sour apple tree and expect to get sweet oranges.

9. If we "take everything off," doesn't that leave us naked (exposed)?

We are only left naked and exposed (vulnerable) when we no longer have protection from God. "Taking everything off" gives our Savior the ability to change us and make us new creations. Being vulnerable is not easy. God sees everything we do, both the good and the bad. He knows all of our hidden secrets. If we are to live our lives the way God wants us to we will be incapable of doing it in our own strength; we must rely on God's hand upon our lives to survive.

CHAPTER 6

BASIC SOLDIER SKILLS

Now all things are of God, who has reconciled us to himself
through Jesus Christ,
and has given us the ministry of reconciliation,
Now then, we are ambassadors for Christ,
as though God were pleading through us;
be reconciled to God.
For he made him who knew no sin to be sin for us,
that we might become the righteousness of God in him.
—2 Corinthians 5:18-21

NEW SOLDIERS FIRST learn skills necessary for survival. Many may apply to both military and civilian life while others apply only in a military context. Basic skills are the building blocks. Military recycling is going through basic training again because we are unable to master the skills necessary to graduate. It is important for us not to have to relearn basic skills like rifle marksmanship, grenade throwing accuracy, and enemy vehicle recognition. In the Bible God delivered the Israelites out of slavery in Egypt and they began their journey to the Promised Land. Unprepared to enter, they wandered around in the desert for the next forty years.

On a warm fall day, halfway through basic training, I was standing in formation with about a hundred other soldiers. One moment I was really hot, the next moment freezing cold. When I asked if I could sit down, the drill sergeant yelled at me. I did not want to make a scene but was really sick and needed help. A couple minutes later I started feeling a very sharp pain in my side. Then the lights went out and I collapsed. Several drill sergeants and my commanding officer ran over while I gasped for air. They lifted me into a pickup and rushed me to the hospital. I had pneumonia. My burning fever took hours to get under control. After four days in the hospital I was still very weak. An officer came into my hospital room and told me I had to make a choice. I could pick up where my company left off and finish with them starting tomorrow, or I could take my time, get better, and be recycled, which, meant I would start over from day one. I chose to rejoin my unit. No one wants to be recycled.

It is better to keep moving forward rather than start all over. We refer to becoming a Christian as being "born again." If this is a redo, a fresh start, then maybe we should consider how to do it (life) better this time. God's ways are significantly different than our ways. Scripture is the owner's manual for humankind, giving us guidance when starting to build our spiritual house (life).

> Therefore whoever hears these sayings of mine, and does them, I will liken him to a wise man who built his house on the rock: and the rain descended, the floods came, and the winds blew and beat on that house; and it did not fall, for it was founded

on the rock. But everyone who hears these sayings of Mine, and does not do them, will be like a foolish man who built his house on the sand: and the rain descended, the floods came, and the winds blew and beat on that house; and it fell. And great was its fall." And so it was, when Jesus had ended these sayings, that the people were astonished at his teaching, for he taught them as one having authority, and not as the scribes.

—Matthew 7:24-29

We gain further perspective when we compare this Scripture passage to another one found in Luke.

Whoever comes to me, and hears my sayings and does them, I will show you whom he is like: He is like a man building a house, who dug deep and laid the foundation on the rock. And when the flood arose, the stream beat vehemently against that house, and could not shake it, for it was founded on the rock. But he who heard and did nothing is like a man who built a house on the earth without a foundation, against which the stream beat vehemently; and immediately it fell. And the ruin of that house was great.

—Luke 6:47-49

We had been up all night marching twenty-five miles in from our final field training exercise. Fatigue and exhaustion set in. We were too tired to care about anything, and it felt wonderful to be back in our barracks. But the training was not over. We assembled in a hot gymnasium and were kept busy with timed drills, taking apart and putting our M-16 machine guns together. A civilian speaker interrupted and talked to us about a bunch of boring uninteresting subjects. A soldier across the room nodded off to sleep. The drill sergeants swarmed in upon him, screaming. I was so glad not to be him! In the aftermath, they removed his chair and he was forced to stand for the remainder of the classes. Fearing the wrath of the drill sergeants, we all resisted sleep.

In a similar fashion, we ought to adjust our lives to please God. His ways are much different than ours.

Seek the Lord while he may be found, call upon him while he is near; let the wicked forsake their way, and the unrighteous their thoughts; let them return to the Lord, that he may have mercy on them, and to our God, for he will abundantly pardon. For my thoughts are not your thoughts, nor are your ways my ways, says the Lord. For as the heavens are higher than the earth, so are my ways higher than your ways and my thoughts than your thoughts.

—Isaiah 55:6-11

1. What does it mean to "build your life upon the Rock"?

This means that those who hear God's words and put them into practice allow God to participate in the building process of our lives. The foundation upon which we build determines all future stability and longevity of the building. There is no foundation more certain than God. If we build upon God's foundation we have nothing to fear. Why are we afraid if we have the God of this universe in control of our lives, knowing that when we die we will have eternal life with him?

2. Who or what is the Rock?

Jesus is "the Rock."

The Lord lives! Blessed be my rock! Let God be exalted, the rock of my salvation!

—2 Samuel 22:47

3. The foolish person builds on the sand. What does sand represent?

Those who do not hear God's words and put them into practice are foolish; they are building their lives according to the world's ways, represented by sand in Scripture. The world would have us believe that money will make us happy. But many rich people are alone and miserable. Maybe power is what we must seek after.

No. The more we try to control our lives the more out of control we become. The more we build our lives upon the sand the more we believe we can save ourselves. Foolish people go to eternal damnation (hell) believing they do not need God. Building on anything but God is a flawed foundation that will crumble into ruin when bad weather comes.

> For we are God's fellow workers; you are God's field, you are God's building. According to the grace of God which was given to me, as a wise master builder I have laid the foundation, and another builds on it. But let each one take heed how he builds on it. For no other foundation can anyone lay than that which is laid, which is Jesus Christ.
> —1 Corinthians 3:9-11

4. What preparation does the wise person make before beginning to build?

Wise people dig down deep, laying a foundation secured on the Rock. We must allow God access to every part of our inner selves. This deep foundation starts at our core (our hearts and minds) building up and out to our words and deeds.

5. What is the foolish person's response to Jesus' words?

It is not wise to imagine ourselves smarter than God. The very best we can do has no eternal value if it is done without God. Throughout our lifelong training we are given opportunities to succeed. God does not want us to fail. The foolish person declares, "There is no God; I don't need anyone to help me succeed!"

> Now if anyone builds on this foundation with gold, silver, precious stones, wood, hay, straw, each one's work will become clear; for the day will declare it, because it will be revealed by fire; and the fire will test each one's work, of what sort it is. If anyone's work which he has built on it endures, he will receive a reward. If anyone's work is burned, he will suffer loss; but he himself

will be saved, yet so as through fire. Do you not know that you are the temple of God and that the Spirit of God dwells in you? If anyone defiles the temple of God, God will destroy him. For the temple of God is holy, which temple you are.

—1 Corinthians 3:12-17

6. What lies ahead for someone who chooses to build upon another foundation?

If we base our lives on something other than God we run the risk of a lifetime of pain and bondage to sin. In the end we may also lose our eternal life in heaven. This is not worth the risk. Build your foundation upon the rock, Jesus. Like soil in a garden, the condition of our hearts determine the amount of growth God's words will have when planted into us. The "Parable of the Sower" describes the categories of heart soils; the seed is the Word of God and the soil is a person's heart.

> A planter went out to sow his seed. And as he sowed, some fell by the wayside; and it was trampled down, and the birds of the air devoured it. Some fell on rock; and as soon as it sprang up, it withered away because it lacked moisture. And some fell among thorns, and the thorns sprang up with it and choked it. But others fell on good ground, sprang up, and yielded a crop a hundredfold. Now the parable is this: the seed is the word of God. Those by the wayside are the ones who hear; then the devil comes and takes away the word out of their hearts, lest they should believe and be saved. But the ones on the rock are those who, when they hear, receive the word with joy; and these have no root, who believe for a while and in time of temptation fall away. Now the ones that fell among thorns are those who, when they have heard, go out and are choked with cares, riches, and pleasures of life, and bring no fruit to maturity. But the ones that fell on the good ground are those who, having heard the word with a noble and good heart, keep it and bear fruit with patience.
>
> —Luke 8:5-15

7. The first soil is the road most travelled.

The road most travelled is the hard ground, the highway or asphalt where the seed simply cannot grow. This soil illustrates a person who hears but does not understand what is being said. What causes someone not to understand? What breaks down our communication with God? Poor communication is one cause. When we talk too much and listen too little our soil is hard. Another cause is translating the message poorly. When there is a barrier between the message and the speaker, the message is confusing. Third, poor listening occurs when we jump ahead to the solution while the speaker is still talking or we say, "I know." Distractions, timing, and lack of focus distort the message. Trying to have an important conversation during a football game is an example of this.

Looking at the world around us and the global Church, it is obvious people do not understand the *Word of God*. We consider the United States to be a Christian nation since its inception but "One Nation under God" is frayed, tattered, and worn, unraveling more with each passing day. Do we understand more about God today than when we first enlisted in his Army? If not, there is a communication breakdown.

God is not failing on his part to communicate with us. If we are not careful, our adversary will snatch our good seed like a hungry flock of birds.

8. We refer to the second type of soil as the "stony places."

This is also referred to as "the path." It is not the main road but is commonly used for foot traffic. The road most travelled would be like a freeway and the path like a small street or sidewalk. We hear the message with great joy. There is excitement but we lack the ability to apply it to our lives. Feeling left alone we think God and others have deserted us. The plant (person) is only able to endure for a short period of time. There is energy but no follow through. This person immediately stumbles. The sun scorches the plant and it withers and dies. No spiritual growth happens in the gravel beside the road where everyone walks. Spiritual growth is like a flash in the pan; it sizzles and pops but there is no substance.

"The road to hell is paved with good intentions."
—Author unknown

The apostle Paul suffered many things for his faith in Christ. He spoke of all he endured for his faith to the Corinthian church.

Are they Hebrews? So am I. Are they Israelites? So am I. Are they the seed of Abraham? So am I. Are they ministers of Christ?—I speak as a fool—I am more: in labors more abundant, in stripes above measure, in prisons more frequently, in deaths often. From the Jews five times I received forty stripes minus one. Three times I was beaten with rods; once I was stoned; three times I was shipwrecked; a night and a day I have been in the deep; in journeys often, in perils of waters, in perils of robbers, in perils of my own countrymen, in perils of the Gentiles, in perils in the city, in perils in the wilderness, in perils in the sea, in perils among false brethren; in weariness and toil, in sleeplessness often, in hunger and thirst, in fasting often, in cold and nakedness, besides the other things, what comes upon me daily: my deep concern for all the churches. Who is weak, and I am not weak? Who is made to stumble, and I do not burn with indignation.
—2 Corinthians 11:22-29

Paul spent at least six years in prison throughout his ministry including Philippi (49 AD), Caesarea (58 AD) and Rome (67 AD), where he was later executed. Paul was preserved by God's power throughout. Beaten, pelted with rocks, shipwrecked, endangered journeys, lacking sleep, food, and water, being cold and even stripped of his clothing were common occurrences during his ministry years. He had plenty of opportunities to turn away from the Lord, but he persevered.

I know that all God's commands are spiritual, but I'm not. Isn't this also your experience? I've spent a long time in sin's prison. What I don't understand about myself is that I decide one way, but then I act another, doing things I absolutely despise. So if I can't be trusted to figure out what is best for myself and then do it, it becomes obvious that God's guidance is necessary. For if I know the laws of God (Scripture) but still can't keep them, and if the power of sin within me keeps sabotaging my best intentions; I obviously need help! I realize that I don't have what it takes. I can will it, but I can't do it. I decide to do good, but I don't really do it; I decide not to do bad, but then I do it anyway. My decisions, such as they are, don't result in actions. Something has gone wrong deep within me and gets the better of me every time.

—Romans 7:14-20 The Message

Sound familiar? Seeds falling on stony ground struggle to survive. Sin is missing the mark. Are we too carnal and not spiritual enough? We must judge ourselves or we risk the judgment of God.

9. The third type of soil is full of thorns.

The farmer never knows when thorns will spring up. He is planting in the same place as years before and invariably thorns will gain root. We come to Christ with our unique experiences, personality traits, and thoughts. These choke out our faith if we are not careful. We must take offensive actions against communication breakdowns. Acting upon what we hear is like applying spiritual Weed-Be-Gone to the weeds, the sins in our lives. Weeds will keep cropping up so cultivation is an ongoing process. If we want godliness we need to keep weeding in the field we have planted. We cannot continue doing the same things and expect different results.

Post this at all the intersections of your heart, dear friends: Lead with your ears, follow up with your tongue, and let anger straggle along in the rear. God's righteousness doesn't grow from human anger. So throw all spoiled virtue and cancerous evil in the garbage. In simple humility, let your gardener, God, landscape, cultivate your life with the Word, making a salvation-garden of your life, where all good things will grow. Don't fool yourself into thinking that you are a listener when you are faking it, letting the Word go in one ear and out the other. Act on what you hear!

Those who hear and don't act are like those who glance in the
mirror, walk away, and two minutes later have no idea who they
are, what they look like. But whoever catches a glimpse of the
revealed counsel of God—the free life, even out of the corner of
his eye, and sticks with it, is no distracted scatterbrain but a man
or woman of action. That person will find delight and affirmation
from the Lord.

—James 1:21-25 The Message

When life gets tough we cannot give up on the race. Pressures,
trials, and troubles can rob us of our joy and leave us broken and use-
less if we allow it. Do not let this happen. Everyone will face sorrow
in their lives. There is a time for everything. The key is keeping our
heads up when life gets difficult. Do not be afraid to mourn. Giving
up does not make us stronger but fighting always will.

10. The fourth type of soil is good and rich, and ready for growing a harvest.

Good soil is symbolic of those who listen and immediately
apply the knowledge to their lives. We grow today and continue
growing until harvest time. The harvester, God, reaps the output
of the crop he desires.

Now to Him who is able to do exceedingly abundantly above all
that we ask or think, according to the power that works in us,
to Him be glory in the church by Christ Jesus to all generations,
forever and ever. Amen.

—Ephesians 3:20-21

Good ground is not perfect but it is healthy. God breaks up,
maintains, and fertilizes the soil to make it ready to receive the
seeds of righteousness. Are we cradling the precious seed? Are
we holding onto the seed in our pockets? Are we encouraging the
seed to grow by watering it? Is the seed getting light from the sun?
Spiritually speaking, this light comes from the Son of God. How
many harvests really bear fruit? How many seasons pass while we

are still believers? The growing cycle during all four seasons of the year applies annually. When was the last time a harvest occurred in our lives? Bearing fruit in the past is great, but has the next growing season begun? God, the gardener, will prune our branches to allow a greater harvest. This is an unpleasant but necessary experience.

A co-worker asked a woman, "What is it like to be a Christian?" The co-worker replied, "It is like being a pumpkin. God picks you from the patch, brings you in, and washes all the dirt off. He cuts off the top and scoops out all the yucky stuff. He removes the seeds of doubt, hate, and greed. He carves us a new face, putting his light inside us for the whole world to see." (Author unknown)

CHAPTER 7

INTERNALIZING GOD'S CORE VALUES

If God is for us, who can be against us?
—Romans 8:31b

…we are more than conquerors through
Him who loves us.
—Romans 8:37

WITH CHRIST IN our hearts the war for our souls is won. When we die we will be with God in heaven for eternity. But while we live on this earth there are still battles we must fight. Does our decision to follow Christ affect our actions?

Receiving care packages was a welcome respite from the daily grind of Basic Training. I received a big box the morning before going out onto the daytime land navigation course. My mother had sent me a batch of cookies and candy for Halloween. The drill sergeant delivering my mail smiled and said, "You do not get to take the box to your room and may not bring it with you. You have five minutes to get rid of it or it will be thrown away." I quickly distributed my treasure among my peers in my platoon. Even the people who barely spoke to me before suddenly became my friends. Wow, what a ravenous lot when homemade cookies are being offered. Having been without home cooking for awhile made us all miss our moms and all the stuff she always does for us.

> Blessed are those who hunger and thirst for righteousness, for they will be filled.
>
> —Matthew 5:6

Until we are really hungry or thirsty, we probably do not put much thought into what we eat or where it comes from. Someone else busily provides for our needs. Craving God as a lifesaving resource allows him access to our lives. He comes to shape and transforms us. The joy in our lives on earth depends on this transformation process. Get hungry! Get thirsty! Go after God like you cannot live without him. You will get much more than just a full belly.

The Bible says we are "created in the image of God" (Gen. 1:27). We do not physically have the same appearance as God since our creator does not have a body. In Colossians 1:15, Paul calls Jesus the "image of the invisible God, the firstborn over all creation." In what way are we created in God's image? Angels are eternal beings and are not created in God's image so this is not a reference to being eternal. God does not have a physical body so it is not a physical reference either. It is not intellectual capacity because the devil and his minions are far superior to humans intellectually.

Our souls or spirits are a reflection of God. In Ecclesiastics 7:29, Solomon writes, "God made man upright." Because of original sin humanity became tainted but God gives humankind the ability to understand divine things and communicate with him.

In a *USA Today* article, September 2006, *View of God can predict values, politics*, Cathy Lynn Grossman states that 91.8% of Americans believe in God. How many of these Americans live a life pleasing to God? Very few who say they are believers allow themselves to be changed. If nearly 92% of our society did believe in and allowed God to guide their lives, we would see a much different world. People call themselves believers but take no action to increase their knowledge and understanding of the One they believe in.

Going to church is something society deems to be of value. As long as we attend church there is a perception of spirituality. There can also be a misconception about what it means to nourish a deeper relationship. Poor examples of what being spiritual means can deter people from digging deeper. Actually, only a deepening understanding of spiritual truth will bring about change. For us to become more like God we cannot continue to live in our present state.

While in college I liked to play basketball during open gym times. After a few weeks of being treated unfairly I stopped going. A group of guys was not allowing everyone else a chance to play. What further exasperated me was the fact that these guys were all studying to be ministers. In some people there seems to be a complete disconnect between morality (following the rules) and ethics (doing what is right).

Americans have differing views on the nature of God: 32% view God as authoritative and angry, 28% as distant and uncaring, and 16% as critical and judgmental. Only 24% view God as benevolently capable of setting absolute standards for our society.

Soldiers are given a new values system upon entry into the military. This value system, the Seven Army Core Values, is designed to supersede all past values. A bit of a romantic idea, still this value system becomes our new morality; it is the standard by which soldiers are to measure what is right and wrong. In a very similar manner, those who become believers in Christ are supposed to adhere to a new standard for living. The standards are not created by man but written within Scripture. The Bible is a guidebook for how we ought to live. Sadly, there are many believers who become casualties of war because they are unwilling to align themselves to God's ways. If we do not apply the Bible to our everyday lives, do what he commands, and allow the church to pour into our lives, it is easy to get off track, becoming injured, snared, or trapped by Satan.

The choice is ours. Slave or free. Our world is desperate for the light. Will we be God's representative and share the truth with others? We have the answer to the most important question in life: is there life after death? Jesus' death ensures us of our eternal destiny. Since God paid the ransom for our souls, why are we not sharing this with everyone around us?

> Walk in the Spirit, and you shall not fulfill the lust of the flesh.
> —Galatians 5:16

1. What does it mean to "walk in the spirit"?

Walking implies moving from one place to another suggesting the idea of reaching a final destination. The "Spirit" is the Holy Spirit of God who lives in all believers. To walk in the spirit is to immerse ourselves in God, allowing him to lead us to our final destination. We do not focus on our physical existence but rather on the invisible world and the things of God. We live a Christ-centered life, not just on Sunday but daily. God encourages us to involve him in our daily lives. Jesus said, "I am the vine and you are the branches, he who abides in me and I in him bear much fruit" (John 15:5).

2. Are the "works of the flesh" things Christians should be doing?

No. The Bible says "our hearts are wicked and our will is set against God" (Jer. 17:9). We all make mistakes. But when we walk in the flesh we make selfish decisions, focusing only on what feels good in the moment without any consideration of consequences for our actions. We must focus on living a life that pleases and reflects God. God does not change us instantaneously but most often rather slowly over time. Our spirits seek fellowship with our Maker. We are living sacrifices. When we try to do it ourselves the discomfort and fear of failure will force us into corrective actions. We must continually depend on his guidance or we will look just like the world.

3. Lists within Scripture, like the one in Galatians 5:17-21, are not all inclusive, but they help us gather a more thorough description of the acts of the sinful nature.

The activities mentioned in Galatians 5 may be visible within the lives of believers, and are counter-productive to spirituality and corporate spiritual development. The following words are even further clarified as transliterated from the original Greek. We must work to diligently find and remove the vile nature of unchecked sin in our lives.

> For the flesh lusts against the Spirit, and the Spirit against the flesh; and these are contrary to one another, so that you do not do the things that you wish. But if you are led by the Spirit, you are not under the law. Now the works of the flesh are evident, which are: adultery, fornication, uncleanness, lewdness, idolatry, sorcery, hatred, contentions, jealousies, outbursts of wrath, selfish ambitions, dissensions, heresies, envy, murders, drunkenness, revelries, and the like; of which I tell you beforehand, just as I also told you in time past, that those who practice such things will not inherit the kingdom of God.
> —Galatians 5:17-21

Adultery (*moicheia*) is voluntary sexual intercourse between a married person and someone other than the one they are legally married to.

You shall not commit adultery.

—Exodus 20:14

Fornication (*porneia*) is illicit sexual intercourse in general, and premarital sex where neither party is married.

Flee fornication. Every sin that a man does is with the body; but he who commits fornication sins against his own body.

—1 Corinthians 6:18

Uncleanness (*akatharsia*) is thinking, saying, or responding with approval to lewd conversation or gestures. It is living impurity of lustful, luxurious, uncontrolled living.

Woe to you, scribes and Pharisees, hypocrites! For you are like whitewashed tombs, which outwardly appear beautiful, but within are full of dead people's bones and all uncleanness.

—Matthew 23:27

Lewdness (*aselgeia*) is an exaggerated and imbalanced preoccupation with sex. It is speaking in an ungodly, worldly manner, encouraging others to turn away from rather than toward God. It is excessive, immoderation in anything, *unbridled lust, licentiousness, lasciviousness, wantonness, outrageousness, shamelessness, and insolence.*

You will bear the consequences of your lewdness and your detestable practices, declares the Lord.

—Ezekiel 16:48

Idolatry (*eido lolatreia*) is interacting with a created thing while ascribing godlike abilities to it and expectations that this object will be able to affect your situation or circumstances.

Sorcery (*pharmakeia*) is witchcraft, using magical incantations to gain more certain response to your life's questions. Sorcery or magical arts, is often found in connection with idolatry and fostered by it.

Put to death therefore what is earthly in you: sexual immorality, impurity, passion, evil desire and covetousness, which is idolatry.
—Colossians 3:5

Hatred (*echthria*) is enmity, not loving one another, despising or shunning, not only wanting to get away from another but wishing ill will upon your adversary.

He who hides hatred has lying lips and he who speaks slander is a fool.
—Proverbs 10:18

Contentions (*ereis*) are strife, quarrels, rivalries, being consistently disagreeable, letting everyone know that you are always right.

A brother offended is more unyielding than a strong city, and quarreling is like the bars of a castle.
—Proverbs 18:19

Jealousies (*zloi*) are to boil or seethe within ourselves, a consuming desire that one would falter so you can assume their position. Whether you have little or plenty, you become dissatisfied with what you have and desire to have what someone else has; you deserve it more than they do. You do not consider purchasing an item but rather to take it and leave the other with nothing.

For jealousy makes a man furious and he will not spare when he takes revenge.
—Proverbs 6:34

Outbursts of wrath (*thumoi*) are the turbulent commotion of the mind, rage. It is strife that burns as hot as heat of the fire. They are uncontrolled explosive and destructive fits of rage. When you blow up someone is going to get hurt.

> Better is a dry morsel with quiet than a house full of feasting with strife.
> —Proverbs 17:1

Selfish ambitions (*eritheiai*) are used of those who electioneer for office, courting popular applause by trickery and doing things to promote self so others will look at us.

> But if you have bitter jealousy and selfish ambition in your hearts, do not boast and be false to the truth.
> —James 3:14

Dissensions (*dichostasiai*) are those who choose to stand apart, causing discord and division amongst the group. You know you are right so you cause people to pick sides, telling others that they are either for you or against you.

> Now I beseech you, brethren, to mark them who make dissensions and offences contrary to the doctrine which you have learned, and avoid them.
> —Romans 16:17

Heresies (*haireseis*) promote divisions (arising from opinions) without any formal separation. Presentations of half truths are so smooth that we can't even tell what is fact or fiction. In ecclesiastical terminology, heresies are saying something about God that is not true.

> But there were false prophets also among the people, even as there shall be false teachers among you, who shall bring in destructive heresies, even denying the Lord that bought them, and bring upon themselves swift destruction.
> —2 Peter 2:1

Envy (*phthonoi*) is jealousy of another's success, depreciation of his worth, envy of his excellence, painful or resentful awareness of an advantage enjoyed by another and an insatiable desire to have it for oneself.

He is puffed up with conceit and understands nothing. He has an
unhealthy craving for controversy and for quarrels about words,
which produce envy, dissension, slander, evil suspicions.
—1 Timothy 6:4

Murders (*phonoi*) are metaphorically or literally taking of
another's life, character assassination of another, or to kill one's
reputation.

You have heard that it was said to those of old, "You shall not
murder;" and whoever murders will be liable to judgment.
—Matthew 5:21

Drunkenness (*methai*) is drinking to excess, losing our abilities
to make conscience decisions when choosing between right and
wrong.

But watch yourselves lest your hearts be weighed down with
dissipation and drunkenness and cares of this life, and that day
come upon you suddenly like a trap.
—Luke 21:34

Revelries (*kōmoi*) may be expressed as nocturnal and riotous
processions of half-drunken and frolicking people parading
through the streets. Throwing all caution to the wind, they seek to
gain approval that has otherwise been denied while in an altered,
inebriated state.

And (they) shall receive the reward of unrighteousness, as they
that count it pleasure to revel in the day time. Spots they are and
blemishes, sporting themselves with their own deceptions while
they feast with you.
—2 Peter 2:13

4. What does it mean to "crucify the flesh"?

It means to die to self; to put the earthly man aside and focus
on spiritual things (God).

5. Are we to become conceited, provoke others, or envy one another?

Flee also youthful lusts; but pursue righteousness, faith, love, peace with those who call on the Lord out of a pure heart. But avoid foolish and ignorant disputes, knowing that they generate strife. And a servant of the Lord must not quarrel but be gentle to all, able to teach, patient, in humility correcting those who are in opposition, if God perhaps will grant them repentance, so that they may know the truth, and that they may come to their senses and escape the snare of the devil, having been taken captive by him to do his will.

—2 Timothy 2:22-26

According to 2 Timothy 2:22-26 we are to flee lust and pursue righteousness, and avoid disputes because they generate strife being patient with one another.

Faith is more than a onetime event in our lives. It is an ongoing process requiring a lifelong commitment. To maintain our faith we need to involve God in our daily lives. As we wake every day we thank God for giving us another day. More than simply saying it and forgetting the statement, let us build our relationship with God through reading and studying his Word. In great or small ways, we gain knowledge and understanding by putting into action the things we have been learning within Scripture.

CHAPTER 8

ADVANCED INDIVIDUAL TRAINING

Simon Peter, a bondservant and apostle of Jesus Christ,
to those who have obtained like precious faith with us
by the righteousness of our God and Savior Jesus Christ.
—2 Peter 1:1

WE HAVE BECOME familiar with the basics of faith; now it is
time to move into Advanced Individual Training (AIT). AIT
builds upon everything we have already been learning. We have

become more proficient in the basics so we are ready to move onto more difficult tasks.

In the military, we were given a weekend pass between basic and advanced individual training. We cannot go far but several of us decided to spend our time in the city. A friend, fellow soldier in training, and I each chipped in for a room in a really expensive hotel. We bought food from a grocery store before going to our room. I bought a ton of junk food, including all the chocolate candy and sweets I could find because it is something we are not allowed to have in our barracks. I ate myself sick but it was a wonderful feeling being on such a sugar high. Training twenty-four seven, we had no time to watch movies so we spent a lot of time at the movie theatre across the street from where we were staying. We watched every movie they had. The time went by too fast. Before we knew it we had to go back. We may have had some fun, but it was short lived.

Sin is kind of like that weekend I took with my friend. Sin is fun or no one would be doing it, right? But sin has a very short shelf life. Like sweets and candy, it will rot our spiritual teeth and undermine our spirituality if we are not careful.

> Grace and peace be multiplied to you in the knowledge of God and of Jesus our Lord, as his divine power has given to us all things that pertain to life and godliness, through the knowledge of him who called us by glory and virtue, by which have been given to us exceedingly great and precious promises, that through these you may be partakers of the divine nature, having escaped the corruption that is in the world through lust. But also for this very reason, giving all diligence, add to your faith virtue, to virtue knowledge, to knowledge self-control, to self-control perseverance, to perseverance godliness, to godliness brotherly kindness, and to brotherly kindness love. For if these things are yours and abound, you will be neither barren nor unfruitful in the knowledge of our Lord Jesus Christ. For he who lacks these things is shortsighted, even to blindness, and has forgotten that he was cleansed from his old sins. Therefore, brethren, be even more diligent to make your call and election sure, for if you do

these things you will never stumble; for so an entrance will be supplied to you abundantly into the everlasting kingdom of our Lord and Savior Jesus Christ.

—2 Peter 1:1-11

1. What does it mean to be "partakers of the divine nature"?

Since the Holy Spirit lives within every Christian, the divine nature ought to be visible through our actions and deeds. Though already mentioned in chapters 6-7, please ask yourself if the following characteristics are evident in your life.

- Virtue is moral excellence. It is the ability to make the hard right choice when working through a moral dilemma.
- Knowledge is the ability to apply learned skills to everyday living.
- Self-control is to restrain oneself effecting appropriate actions and feelings.
- Perseverance is to be resolute holding on in following a particular course of action.
- Godliness, beyond moral uprightness is one who actively conforms to the laws and wishes of God.
- Brotherly kindness is expressing appreciation for another's physical presence.
- Love, as a gift from God, cares more about others than oneself. To love is to be a tender, passionate, and affectionate person toward other people.

2. Why does God discipline us?

The writer of Hebrews says;

For whom the Lord loves he chastens, and scourges every son whom he receives. If you endure chastening, God deals with you as with sons; for what son is there whom a father does not chasten? But if you are without chastening, of which all have become partakers, then you are illegitimate and not sons. Furthermore, we have had human fathers who corrected us, and we paid them respect. Shall we not much more readily be in subjection to the father of spirits and live? For they indeed for a few days chastened us as seemed best to them, but he for our profit, that we may be partakers of his holiness. Now no chastening seems to be joyful for the present, but painful; nevertheless, afterward it yields the peaceable fruit of righteousness to those who have been trained by it.

—Hebrews 12:6-11

Discipline may not be pleasant but it is necessary in order to grow and mature in our faith. Much like a pruning process, he disciplines us so we can grow stronger and be able to bear more fruit. Since God only disciplines those whom he loves we ought to view discipline as a necessary reaction to our bad behavior. As we align our lives to his ways our behaviors do not require discipline. We aim to please him at all times. Looking in the mirror at our spirituality is sometimes discouraging. The perfection of God makes our inadequacies obvious, dashing our hopes for being acceptable based upon our own "good works" upon the rocks of despair.

The corrections of God help us to see where we can improve. Here are some additional Scriptures on discipline.

When with rebukes you correct a man for iniquity, you make his beauty melt away like a moth; surely every man is vapor.

—Psalm 39:11

The fear of the Lord is the beginning of knowledge, but fools despise wisdom and instruction.

—Proverbs 1:7

My son, do not despise the chastening of the Lord, nor detest His correction; for whom the Lord loves he corrects, just as a father the son in whom he delights.

—Proverbs 3:11-12

God has not given us a spirit of fear, but of power and of love and of a sound mind.

—2 Timothy 1:7

3. What is the Fruit of the Spirit?

The apostle Paul tells us,

But the fruit of the Spirit is love, joy, peace, longsuffering, kindness, goodness, faithfulness, gentleness, self-control. Against such there is no law. And those who are Christ's have crucified the flesh with its passions and desires. If we live in the Spirit, let us also walk in the Spirit.

—Galatians 5:22-25

Scripture itself defines all the key words from this list.

Love (*agape*) is offered to all without restriction or reservation. You cannot earn it and do not deserve it. Consider God's love as a state of perfect peace. There is not a stir, commotion, or agitation. It is still like a quiet sea or the air without a hint of a breeze. In this state there is no noise or disturbance. Imagine a hushed silence. There is no need to be anxious; there is freedom from the disturbances of noise or alarm, disorder, trouble, and turbulence. God's love is not showy or intended to attract attention. It is like a beautiful mosaic of all the colors and experiences of life.

Keep yourselves in the love of God, waiting for the mercy of our Lord Jesus Christ that leads to eternal life.

—Jude 1:21

Joy (*chara*) is more than just a feeling of ecstatic happiness, pleasure, or satisfaction; it is a certainty that neither plight nor circumstance can derail. An example of this unwavering joy is found in the words of James:

Consider it pure joy, my brothers, whenever you face trials of many kinds, because you know that the testing of your faith develops perseverance. Perseverance must finish its work so that you may be mature and complete, not lacking anything.

—James 1:2-4

Peace (*eirēnē*) is the absence of war or other hostilities. It is free from quarrels and disagreements. Harmonious relations exist in every direction. Publically, all is in order and we feel secure. An inner contentment in contrast with strife rests upon us. Carrying over an Old Testament theme, the Hebrew word *shalom* is certainly still applicable today. This state of health or well-being denotes a state of untroubled, undisturbed well-being. The "peace of God" results in forgiveness enjoyed because of the blood of Jesus Christ. We are free from all anxiety and care knowing our present and future are secured by his power.

And the peace of God, which transcends all understanding, will guard your hearts and your minds in Christ Jesus.

—Philippians 4:7

Longsuffering (*makrothumia*) means to be emotionally in control. We are slow to wrath, exuding a patient endurance.

Strengthened with all might, according to his glorious power, unto all patience and longsuffering with joyfulness.

—Colossians 1:11

Kindness (*chrēstotēs*) is a common human feeling. It is congenial and sympathetic, often considered kindhearted. It shows tenderness or goodness; disposed to do good and confer happiness; averse to hurting or paining; benevolent; benignant; gracious; gentle; tractable; easily governed; as, a horse settles into its harness.

Now may the LORD show steadfast love and faithfulness to you. And I will do good to you because you have done this thing.

—2 Samuel 2:6

Goodness (*agathosune*) is the quality or state of being gentle, mild, benevolent, docile, etc. A tender heart offers a softness of manners, disposition, fairness, and moderation.

> Surely goodness and mercy shall follow me all the days of my life, and I shall dwell in the house of the Lord forever.
> —Psalm 23:6

Faithfulness (*pistis*) is expressed as loyalty. It is a careful and exact observance of duty, an adherence to fidelity, and the discharge of obligations. It is doing what is right for oneself, your family, and community. Honest to a fault, true to your word, firmly fixed upon convictions obtained through knowledge through life experiences and confidence in what we hear from God in his Word.

> Steadfast love and faithfulness preserve the king, and by steadfast love his throne is upheld.
> —Proverbs 20:28

Gentleness (*praotēs*) is quietness, not rough, harsh, or stern. A three pack of characteristics might be mild, meekness, almost bland. A gentle person is not boring, but also not a thrill seeker. The amiable, gentle nature, even temperament, and disposition make interaction with this person palatable for just about anyone. The idea is readily joined together with words like respect, consideration, or conciliation. Tame, not violent or rough, a behind the scenes worker who is not loud or drawing attention to oneself. This is a passive person, as in a gentle touch, smooth and agreeable.

> But as for you... flee these things. Pursue righteousness, godliness, faith, love, steadfastness, gentleness.
> —1 Timothy 6:11

Self-control (*enkrateia*) is an exhibition of power or authority over oneself. It is the ability to check or restrain using a regulating influence, governance, or superintendence. Self-control is mastery or dominion over self (opposite to self-indulgence), the grace by which the flesh or body is controlled.

> A man without self-control is like a city broken into and left without walls.
>
> —Proverbs 25:28

4. Is the Fruit of the Spirit supposed to be kept secret?

No. Every Christian should be fully aware of this fruit and do their best to exhibit God in every capacity of their lives.

CHAPTER 9

DUTIES, RESPONSIBILITIES, ENTITLEMENTS

Then he (Jesus) said to them, "Follow me,
and I will make you fishers of men.
—Matthew 4:19

NOW THAT WE have a foundation of knowledge about what God expects of us, we need to receive our general orders so we know what to do and what to expect from him. In the military, physical training is necessary for soldiers because there are negative consequences to being out of shape and overweight. Beyond that, soldiers are training for battle. To be effective on the battlefield, soldiers must train their bodies to withstand lack of sleep, stress, and physical strain. It is necessary for them to know what their responsibilities are so they can perform assigned tasks with excellence and distinction.

As soldiers in God's Army, we must be trained in spiritual matters; we are training for spiritual battle that can occur anytime, anywhere. What was it that caused you to want to enlist in the Army of God? Did you see something in someone else and say to yourself, *I have got to have some of that?* Did you ask someone about their faith or did someone approach you and share their faith with you? Scripture tells us that God came to live among humankind in the form of Jesus Christ. While on earth, he went out to where the people were and shared the truths of God with everyone he came into contact with. Of those whom he spoke to in this manner he handpicked twelve men. Like all those who came into contact with God, they heard the "Good News" of the Gospel message and needed to decide how to respond. *Do I accept Jesus Christ as my Savior, or do I continue to go my own way?* they thought. For these men, a decision to follow Jesus meant an entire life and occupational change.

Have you already accepted Jesus? What has changed for you? I am not saying that everything has to change completely, nor am I suggesting that everyone has to become an evangelist or preacher. Have you ever been in the presence of God? Have you been in his presence anytime lately? I have heard many people say they experience God during worship services at church. By implication, God has been among us, right? If he has been among us and he is perfect, then I would have to pause to ask you again, how have you been changed?

> Now it was so, when Moses came down from Mount Sinai (and the two tablets of the testimony were in Moses' hand when he came down from the mountain), that Moses did not know that the skin of his face shone while he talked with him. So when Aaron and all the children of Israel saw Moses, behold, the skin of his

face shone, and they were afraid to come near him. Then Moses
called to them, and Aaron and all the rulers of the congregation
returned to him; and Moses talked with them. Afterward all the
children of Israel came near, and he gave them as commandments
all that the Lord had spoken with him on Mount Sinai. And
when Moses had finished speaking with them, he put a veil on
his face. But whenever Moses went in before the Lord to speak
with him, he would take the veil off until he came out; and he
would come out and speak to the children of Israel whatever he
had been commanded.

—Exodus 34:29-34

Moses was changed after being with God. His face radiated so
brightly he had to cover it up so he could carry on his daily business.
Only before God would he drop his veil and speak face-to-face.
There is no faking it; people around us know whether we have
been with God or not. As for me, I want to be changed; I want to
be more like God than I was before.

Too often people wear masks to shield their identities, intentions,
or to protect themselves from the scrutiny of others. Regrettably,
this is true for us as believers as well. It is a learned behavior for self
preservation. Wearing masks is not okay. Particularly with God and
other believers we are to openly share our concerns and thoughts.
Tactfulness is still valuable, though. Knowing what to say and how
to say it requires careful consideration. Sometimes, we just know
what needs to be said. An awareness of the situation might cause
us to hold our tongue until such a time when the other person is
more receptive to our counsel.

Let your conversation be always full of grace, seasoned with salt,
so that you may know how to answer everyone.

—Colossians 4:6

The story of the "fall of humankind" in the Garden of Eden
illustrates why we have such a compelling need to "cover up." The
original man and woman had been created to live in an ecologically
perfect environment. The weather was great. The animals all got

along. They enjoyed a perfect relationship with each other and with God. Adam and Eve's nakedness was not an issue as they felt completely safe and secure. Everything changed, though, after Adam and Eve ate the forbidden fruit.

> Now the serpent was more cunning than any beast of the field which the LORD God had made. And he said to the woman, "Has God indeed said, you shall not eat of every tree of the garden?" And the woman said to the serpent, "We may eat the fruit of the trees of the garden; but of the fruit of the tree which is in the midst of the garden, God has said, "You shall not eat it, nor shall you touch it, lest you die." Then the serpent said to the woman, "You will not surely die. For God knows that in the day you eat of it your eyes will be opened, and you will be like God, knowing good and evil." So when the woman saw that the tree was good for food, that it was pleasant to the eyes, and a tree desirable to make one wise, she took of its fruit and ate. She also gave to her husband with her, and he ate. Then the eyes of both of them were opened, and they knew that they were naked; and they sewed fig leaves together and made themselves coverings.
> —Genesis 3:1-7

The serpent (Satan) was correct in saying their eyes would be open but he left out the part about how much this knowledge was going to cost them. Following Satan's advice actually destroyed every certainty they previously enjoyed. Sin tastes good but will eventually make one sick. Immediately they became self conscious, doubtful, and insecure. Looking at each other through these new eyes they sewed some fig leaves together to cover themselves.

Picking up the story, we find God coming down to walk and talk with his beloved Adam and Eve.

> And they heard the sound of the LORD God walking in the garden in the cool of the day, and Adam and his wife hid themselves from the presence of the LORD God among the trees of the garden. Then God called to Adam and said to him, "Where are you?" So he said, "I heard Your voice in the garden, and I was afraid because I was naked; and I hid myself." And He said, "Who told

you that you were naked? Have you eaten from the tree of which
I commanded you that you should not eat?" Then the man said,
"The woman whom You gave to be with me, she gave me of the
tree, and I ate." And the LORD God said to the woman, "What is
this you have done?" The woman said, "The serpent deceived
me, and I ate."

—Genesis 3:8-13

As God is omniscient (all knowing) he knew where Adam and
Eve were and what they had done. Their response was similar
to what we do today after we mess up. Some say, "I do not go to
church so I will not have to admit my failure." Is God's view of
our lives limited to our church attendance? I think the idea is a
little too naïve. God knows what we do and when we do it. Adam
was afraid of God. How could anyone be afraid of someone who
has provided so much for him? When we sin, guilt and shame are
packaged accessories. The more we try to cover up our sins the
more obvious they become to God and others around us. Have you
ever wondered if what you had just done was sin? There are three
easy ways for us to determine right from wrong. First, even before
the thought becomes an action, God is already speaking to us. The
Holy Spirit (who lives inside of all believers) tries to nudge us in
the right direction. Secondly, we may be able to follow another
Christian's example. Third, Scripture itself might guide us away
from harm or toward a truth.

As a last ditch attempt to get away with their sin Adam started
making up excuses. The blame game started as he said it was all
Eve's fault. Please stop, God said. You are not getting away with
anything. You have disobeyed me and I am going to have to punish
you. God's punishment for Adam and Eve seems harsh and maybe
even extreme. But, we immediately see his provision for eventual
restoration.

The Lord God made tunics of skin, and clothed them.

—Genesis 3:21

Some innocent animals had to be killed in order for Adam and Eve's bodies to be covered. Covering their bodies with the animal skins is a picture of the future sacrificial system for the nation of Israel. By God's design, they needed to sacrifice a spotless, perfect lamb once every year to cover their sins. Today, we are no longer under the animal sacrificial system but God still requires a sacrifice in order for our penalty for sin to be removed from us. Jesus' death was the once-for-all sacrifice for our sins.

> For it is not possible that the blood of bulls and goats could take away sins.
> —Hebrews 10:4

> ...we have been sanctified through the offering of the body of Jesus Christ once for all.
> —Hebrews 10:10

> When Jesus came to John to be baptized, John said,

> Behold, the "Lamb of God" who takes away (covers up) the sins of the world.
> —John 1:29

I believe Adam and Eve are in heaven today, don't you? It was a process for their sins to be forgiven but also their perfect relationship and daily interaction with God was restored. I hope this knowledge helps you to stop trying to hide from God. Step up; take what you deserve and get back to living with God the way he wants you to.

God is speaking to us. When we are in his presence and he speaks to us we are compelled to change. May God help us all to drop our guards before him and others. If wearing a veil is necessary for us to function in daily life, let us look for the opportunities to drop and let the light of God shine through.

Attempting to help his disciples understand how different their lives were going to be with him, Jesus told them many parables. In one such parable while he was talking to some fishermen, he told them they were to become "fishers of men" (Matt. 4:19).

1. What does it mean to be "fishers of men"?

Recognizing who he was talking to, Jesus spoke in terms the disciples could readily understand. Instead of catching fish, Jesus turned their attention to "catching" people. These men, and believers today, need to recognize that God uses people to draw others to him. As believers, he wants us to tell our stories of how we come to believing in him. He wants us to share our experiences, particularly those where we have seen the miraculous hand of God. You might say, "I do not know what to do, or how to lead someone to Christ. I do not want to mess this up." Do not worry—God sets us up to succeed.

> Jesus said, "If I am lifted up from the earth, I will draw all peoples to myself."
> —John 12:32

To witness about God and encourage others to come to him does not require a lot of training. Like the parables about salt and light, it does not take much to make a big difference.

> You are the salt of the earth; but if the salt loses its flavor, how shall it be seasoned? It is then good for nothing but to be thrown out and trampled underfoot by men. You are the light of the world. A city that is set on a hill cannot be hidden. Nor do they light a lamp and put it under a basket, but on a lamp stand, and it gives light to all who are in the house. Let your light so shine before men, that they may see your good works and glorify your Father in heaven.
> —Matthew 5:13-16

2. How does the phrase "we are salt and light unto the world" apply to Christians?

Salt is a preservative and also adds flavor to the food. It only requires a small amount of salt to change the way food tastes. "I am a failure. I have never shared my faith with anyone," you might say. Do not worry; God is not going to throw you away. God is, nevertheless, very committed to saving people from "eternal darkness." If you have not witnessed, you are acting against God's will for all to be saved. Confess this sin to God. In repentance change the direction you are going in. Let the Lord show you what to say and how to say it.

3. What does it mean to "let your light shine"?

The Bible says that, "God lives within us" (1 Jn. 4:12). Like a beacon in a lighthouse, Jesus is the light shining into our darkened world. As such, we can choose whether or not to let his light shine through us. If we were out on the raging sea and saw the light coming from the lighthouse, we would be encouraged and hopeful. All we have to do is follow the light and we will make it safely home. We shine the light into the world, because without Jesus people are lost and will not find their way home.

4. Does Jesus suggest or command Christians to be witnesses?

> And Jesus came and spoke to them, saying, "All authority has been given to me in heaven and on earth. Go, therefore, and make disciples of all the nations, baptizing them in the name of the Father and of the Son and of the Holy Spirit, teaching them to observe all things that I have commanded you; and lo, I am with you always, even to the end of the age.
> —Matthew 28:18-20

Jesus' words are stronger than a subtle suggestion. He told (commanded) his disciples to be witnesses. This passage is often referred to as the "Great Commission." Before being crucified, Jesus shared some important thoughts (new marching orders) with his disciples. He knew they would be afraid after he died. He did not want them to crawl into holes to hide. He reminded them of what he had taught them. Even if he was not with them physically, they needed to continue the mission he was on, the reason why he had come "to seek and save the lost" (Luke 19:10).

5. When are we supposed to be ready to tell others about him?

God expects all of us to be ready to tell others about him at all times.

> But sanctify the Lord God in your hearts, and always be ready to give a defense to everyone who asks you a reason for the hope that is in you, with meekness and fear.
> —1 Peter 3:15

You never know how encouraging your words might be to someone else. It is all right to be afraid, but do not let your fear paralyze you and make you unable to give God glory for what he has done, is doing, and will do in your life.

> Let everything that has breath praise the LORD.
> —Psalm 150:6

6. What should we say when someone asks us about our faith?

When asked about God we give them an honest answer for the hope we have. Upon salvation, we are delivered from the penalty of our past sins. An old song says "the burden has been rolled away." The indwelling Holy Spirit is our constant counselor, friend, and guide into all truth. Our future life and death are secure as we know God is in control. Nothing happens anywhere or anytime without God's permission or direction.

> For we cannot but speak the things which we have seen and heard.
> —Acts 4:20

> So they said, "Believe on the Lord Jesus Christ, and you will be saved, you and your household."
> —Acts 16:31

7. What is the purpose of sharing our thoughts concerning faith?

We share our faith in God so that sinners may come to salvation, and as a testimony to encourage further spiritual growth in others and ourselves. Salvation is a free gift from God. We entrust ourselves to God. Rather than selfishly keeping God to ourselves, we share our experiences and the life changing power and love of God with everyone we can.

> Now then, we are ambassadors for Christ, as though God were pleading through us: we implore you on Christ's behalf, be reconciled to God.
>
> —2 Corinthians 5:20

8. What is an ambassador's job?

An ambassador is a representative who seeks to bring dialogue between two different governments. Ambassadors go to great lengths to break down any resistance to communication. They help clarify what each party is saying and get them to speak the same language, even if it is through an interpreter. Christians are God's ambassadors to a lost world. Having been lost ourselves we know how to communicate with the people. Fear and uncertainty cause others to resist our message. Do not force the issue; wait for the opportunity to speak. Be encouraging. Share the story of why and how you came to accept Jesus as your Savior. Offer hope (a lifeline) to someone who is lost and dying without even knowing it. Considering the alternatives, accepting Christ is the best option. We plead and implore you on Christ's behalf for others to be reconciled to God (1 Cor. 5:19). We work diligently because we know Jesus is the only way to be saved.

CHAPTER 10

NIGHT INFILTRATION AND/OR LAND NAVIGATION

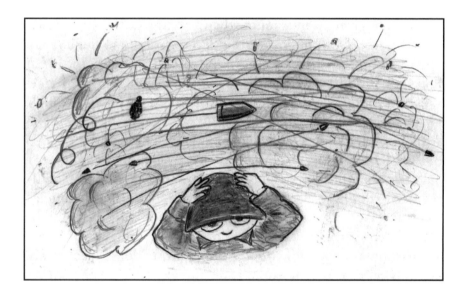

Most assuredly, I say to you, he who believes in me,
the works that I do he will do also;
and greater works than these he will do,
because I go to my father.
—John 14:12

WHEN I WAS in the Army, the Night Infiltration Course and Night Land Navigation were exciting events to see approaching on the horizon. The idea of bullets flying overhead or grenades exploding nearby was intimidating. Though soldiers did not want to get shot at, it was a realistic possibility when going to war. Our natural fear of the dark caused us to be anxious about finding our way during nighttime. Fear of the unknown provoked uncertainty; our imaginations worked to exasperate our fears. Avoidance was an option if we were not going in a particular direction. Fear caused our hearts to race.

Everyone experiences fear, including Christians. But getting beyond our fears makes us stronger. Who are we afraid of letting down? How do we overcome our fears? The two events previously mentioned were designed to help soldiers face and conquer their fears of combat and isolation.

God has given us much more than a secure future. As we train, we recognize we all have something to contribute to the body of Christ, the team, the church. We often feel insignificant; what could I do to assist the team? Maybe they are better off without me. These are simply not words that Christians should use. The Bible says, "We are fearfully and wonderfully made" (Psalms 139:14). Without each of us the Body of Christ is incomplete.

As I look around I see there are a lot of things to do. Surely someone else will do it, right? I have heard that, "Ten percent of the people are doing ninety percent of the work around the church." If this is a true statement, many things are not done because the few workers cannot be everywhere at once. You might say, "I want to work, but do not know what to do or how to do it." Thankfully, the Holy Spirit is here to equip and empower us for service. Jesus is our commanding general but who is the Holy Spirit? He is an equal partner within the Trinity: Father, Son, and Holy Spirit. What does he do? Some quick snapshots through the Scriptures help us understand who the Spirit is and what he does.

During the Creation narrative of Genesis, the Spirit "hovers over the waters" (Genesis 1:2). In the Old Testament, we read of the Spirit coming upon people to complete specific tasks. For instance, in Exodus we read, "the Spirit of God filled a man with wisdom, understanding and knowledge in all manners of workmanship, to design artistic works, to work in gold, in silver, in bronze, in cutting jewels for setting, in carving wood and to work in all manner of workmanship" (Exodus 31:3-5).

1. Is the Holy Spirit indwelling or empowerment only for pastors or a select few?

The Holy Spirit of the Old Testament came upon people for a specific event or season, then would depart until his Presence or power was needed again. While leading the Israelites out of Egypt and across the desert, Moses reached the end of his ability to care for the people. In the book of Numbers God instructs Moses to,

> Gather seventy men of the elders of Israel. Bring them to the tabernacle of meeting with you. I will come down and talk with you there. I will take of the Spirit that is upon you and will put the same upon them; and they shall bear the burden of the people with you, that you may not bear it yourself alone.
> —Numbers 11:16-17

Balaam is an example of the Spirit coming upon an unrighteous man to fulfill God's purposes. We read that "the Spirit of God came upon him" (Num. 24:2).

Moses' successor, Joshua son of Nun, was said to have been "full of the spirit of wisdom" (Deut. 34:9).

The frequency of the Spirit's activity among the people of Israel increased dramatically among the lives of the prophets Elijah (1 Kings 18:12) and Elisha (2 Kings 2:15).

The Spirit frequently came upon and empowered political leaders and even military commanders. The Spirit came upon each of the judges (Judges 3:10; 6:34; 11:29; 13:25; 14:6; 14:19; 15:14), King Saul (1 Samuel 10:6), King David (1 Samuel 16:13, 14, 23; 19:20), and the military commander, Amasi (1 Chronicles 12:18).

Having the Spirit upon us does not give us a license to sin, or place us above divine supervision.

> The Spirit of God came upon Azariah. And he went out to meet Asa (the king of Israel) and said to him: "The Lord is with you while you are with him. If you seek him, he will be found by you; but if you forsake him, he will forsake you."
> —2 Chronicles 15:1-2

The Spirit offers encouragement when the battle approaches.

Then the Spirit of the Lord came upon Jahaziel in the midst of the
assembly. The Lord says to you: "Do not be afraid nor dismayed,
for the battle is not yours, but God's."
—2 Chronicles 20:13, 15

The Spirit came upon King Jehoiada, bringing a firm warning,
a precursor to coming judgment.

The Spirit of God came upon Zechariah, and said to them, "Why
do you transgress the commandments of the Lord, so that you
cannot prosper? Because you have forsaken the Lord, he also
has forsaken you."
—2 Chronicles 24:20

In the troughs of battle, the Spirit rallies the troops, holding up
a guerdon of victory and hope.

When the enemy comes in like a flood, the Spirit of the Lord will
lift up a standard against him.
—Isaiah 59:19

The Spirit came upon Ezekiel on eleven different occasions
(Ezekiel 2:2; 3:12, 14, 24; 8:3; 10:17; 11:1, 5, 24; 37:1; 43:5).

Early in the New Testament writings, the Spirit interacted with
Jesus (landing upon him) in a similar fashion as he had in Old
Testament days: "and he saw the Spirit of God descending like a
dove and landing upon him" (Matthew 3:16).

Near the end of Jesus' life, he shared some important thoughts
about the new, more permanent indwelling of the Spirit. All believers can now enjoy an ongoing interaction with the Spirit.

The Spirit of truth will guide you into all truth; for he will not
speak on his own authority, but whatever he hears he will speak;
and he will tell you things to come. He will glorify me, for he
will take of what is mine and declare it to you. All things that the

father has are mine. Therefore, I said that he will take of mine
and declare it to you.

—John 16:13-15

After the death and resurrection of Christ, Jesus appeared
among them to calm their fears. Fulfilling his previous teachings,
he breathed on them and they received the indwelling of the Holy
Spirit. In this instance, the Spirit simultaneously indwelt all of
them. Wow, we now have direct access to the divine!

> Then, the same day at evening, being the first day of the week, when
> the doors were shut where the disciples were assembled, for fear
> of the Jews, Jesus came and stood in the midst, and said to them,
> "Peace be with you." When he had said this, he showed them his
> hands and his side. Then the disciples were glad when they saw the
> Lord. So Jesus said to them again, "Peace to you! As the Father has
> sent me, I also send you." And when he had said this, he breathed
> on them, and said to them, "Receive the Holy Spirit."
>
> —John 20:19-22

The indwelling happens at the moment of conversion, when
we accept Christ as Savior. By inference today we can easily apply
the name "Immanuel" to the Spirit and truly say that "God is with
us" all the time.

2. What role do people around us play in matters of faith?

We are "surrounded by a great cloud of witnesses." Those who
went before us and everyone around us are watching what we do.
Everything we do is to bring glory unto God. Therefore,

> Let us lay aside every weight, and the sin which so easily ensnares
> us, and let us run with endurance the race that is set before us,
> looking unto Jesus, the author and finisher of our faith, who for
> the joy that was set before Him endured the cross, despising the
> shame, and has sat down at the right hand of the throne of God.
>
> —Hebrews 12:1-2

In like manner, we are to be an example of faith to those around us.

3. Who will have the greatest impact upon us while we are here on earth?

Hopefully, people of genuine faith will have the greatest impact. But, many others—believers and unbelievers, world renowned public figures and athletes, international and national politicians, locally known teachers, coaches, supervisors, peers, and subordinates—will also impact our lives. Obviously, there are a myriad of people who influence us.

4. What does it mean to "stir up the gift of God"?

This means to make the gift of God manifest (evident) in our lives so that others see what is within you. The phrase, stir up (found in the KJV) is a reference to the act of preparing a meal. Adding seasonings to the stew is a great start, but mixing them in is a critical step. All the seasonings simply sink to the bottom unless they are stirred up. The same phrase (from the New International Version) tells us to "fan to flame" of the gift of God. This idea develops a picture of simply adding more wood to a diminishing fire and fanning the coals so the fire will continue to burn, offering light and heat.

5. What could cause a person's faith to burn low and begin to fade?

Fear of what people might think is one way in which people's faith burns low. We are too concerned about what others think. Fear of failure makes us unable to see personal significance and hope for the future, causing the flame of faith to fade. Our regrets of past failures make us feel unworthy to receive God's love.

6. What kind of Spirit has God given us?

God has not given us a spirit of fear, but of power and of love
and of a sound mind.

—2 Timothy 1:7

God has provided us with an antidote for overcoming fear when
it threatens to paralyze us. Christians are called the "children of
God;" we are given access to God's love. This love is beyond human
egocentric needs. With grateful hearts we reverence the living God.
We act with an awareness of God's watchful care and direction. The
sound mind he gives us creates within us the ability to reason and
resolve physical, mental, and moral dilemmas. Submission to order
and control makes the best sense. We train together under orders,
maximizing our regular and systematic actions while building
habits of obedience.

7. Why was the apostle Paul's declaration, "I am not ashamed" such a dynamic statement?

Paul once said he was "chief among the sinners" (1 Timothy
1:15). Like all of us he was not perfect. Rather than boasting on
past successes he did not "think of himself more highly than he
ought to think but soberly." "God has dealt to each one a measure
of faith." Since, "all the members do not have the same function, so
we, being many, are one body in Christ, and individually members
of one another." (Romans 12:3-5). A restored relationship with God
may not eliminate the consequences of past actions but like Paul we
can certainly say I am persuaded that he who began a good work
in me is faithful to complete it (Philippians 1:6). Believers move
forward through training and life with a confidence knowing that
God is on their side. We are constantly looking forward to where
God is taking us.

CHAPTER 11

GRADUATION DAY

I beseech you therefore, brethren, by the mercies of God, that
you present your bodies a living sacrifice, holy, acceptable to
God, which is your reasonable service.
And do not be conformed to this world,
but be transformed by the renewing of your mind,
that you may prove what is that good and acceptable and
perfect will of God.
—Romans 12:1-2

BEFORE WE COULD graduate from basic military training, they took us on a five mile run. We were told to finish this run in less than forty-five minutes or we would not be allowed to graduate. Though we had run a lot in training we had not run this far, this was by far the worse. My lungs burned and my legs felt like rubber. My body ached under the strain of the pace. I kept telling myself *if others can do it I can too*. We all finished. No one fell out of formation. We finished in forty minutes, and we all graduated together.

Graduation is a big event in the Army. On my graduation day, we stood on a huge parade field observed by the commanding generals. We could not look around so I could only spot them from my peripheral vision. There were thousands of soldiers on the field, countless more than I thought there were. As the ceremony concluded I realized I made it; I survived basic training and could now go home for a couple weeks before going to my permanent duty station.

Christians must also leave basic training. The writer of Hebrews tells us that we ought "go on and get past the elementary stage in the teachings and doctrine of Christ (the Messiah), advancing steadily toward the completeness and perfection that belong to spiritual maturity" (Hebrews 6:1 AMP). It is time to serve. But, where do we go from here? Life is an unknown journey; what should we pack? The rigors of training may have become more comfortable than the possibilities of stepping out in faith into the great unknown.

As the Body of Christ, we all contribute to our overall direction. We decide where to live, what job to have, and the relationships we make. Now that training is over, we must maintain what we have gained.

If you do not know exactly what you are going to do, you will have some extra time on your hands so you need to do some forward planning, thinking of ways to fill that time with productive activities, like college, exercise, hobbies, games, reading, and relationships. Ultimately, no one is completely in control of their future, so you need to focus upon the idea of blooming wherever you are planted. Scripture speaks about faith as an ongoing activity.

The more time you spend with God the more you get to know and appreciate him. Before taking another step, pause and say to God, "I present myself to you and your service." Praise the Lord! You have been transformed from casual Christian spectators into a valuable contributor to the cause of Christ.

1. What does it mean to "present our bodies as living sacrifices to God"?

It means to die to self and let God have his way with us.

> I have been crucified with Christ and I no longer live, but Christ lives in me. The life I now live in the body, I live by faith in the Son of God, who loved me and gave himself for me.
> —Galatians 2:20

2. What does it mean to be "transformed by the renewing of our minds"?

This means we need to take every thought captive; we cannot continue to allow carnal thoughts to outweigh the presence of God.

> For those who live according to the flesh set their minds on the things of the flesh, but those who live according to the Spirit, the things of the Spirit. For to be carnally minded is death, but to be spiritually minded is life and peace. Because the carnal mind is enmity against God; for it is not subject to the law of God, nor indeed can be. So then, those who are in the flesh cannot please God.
> —Romans 8:5-8

3. What does it mean to have "a mind set on the things of the flesh"?

This means we have worldly, ungodly thinking that is nothing but self-gratification. Everything I do I do for myself.

4. Are those whose minds are fleshly able to please God?

No. They cannot.

> Do not love the world or the things in the world. If anyone loves
> the world, the love of the Father is not in him. For all that is in
> the world—the lust of the flesh, the lust of the eyes, and the pride
> of life—is not of the Father but is of the world.
>
> —1 John 2:15-16

5. What does it mean to "love the world"?

To love the world is to put worldly things above our relationship
with God. God does not want us to worry about our lives. He is in
control. Since the God of the universe is in charge we have nothing
to fear. This does not mean we always get our way, or that all we
have to do is pray and everything will fit perfectly together. God
loves us and will allow challenges so we can grow.

6. What does "lust" mean?

Lust is an intense sexual desire or appetite. This appetite is
out of bounds and without restraint. As with anything in life, it is
taking something healthy to excess and making it destructive. This
is not a desire for something we are meant to have. Sexual desire
within a marriage relationship is not only healthy but productive.
Even in this sense, if we elevate our relationship higher than God
the potential to harm us is there.

> Do you not know that friendship with the world is enmity with
> God? Whoever therefore wants to be a friend of the world makes
> himself an enemy of God.
>
> —James 4:4

7. Are you an enemy of God or an ally?

Scripture clearly states there is no middle ground (1 John
4:6). We are either for God or against him. When we pledge our

allegiance, he determines to be there with us in times of great need and peril. We are not to slander or speak negatively about our commander. Everything we say must bring him praise and honor. We support our Savior, spiritual leadership, president, government, country, state, local community, friends, family, and even our enemies. It is easy to tear down but much harder to strengthen others.

8. What are believers supposed to think about? Why?

The Bible tells us that warfare is waged in the mind (see 2 Corinthians 10:4-5; Proverbs 23:7), so it's important to guard our thought life. The apostle Paul tells us,

> Finally, brethren, whatever things are true, whatever things are noble, whatever things are just, whatever things are pure, whatever things are lovely, whatever things are of good report, if there is any virtue and if there is anything praiseworthy—meditate on these things.
>
> —Philippians 4:8

We think about God and godliness to help keep ourselves from getting spiritually off track. If left to our own thoughts we are easily distracted. Slowly but surely God is changing us.

9. What is the armor of God? (see also Gal. 5:22-23)

> Therefore take up the whole armor of God, that you may be able to withstand in the evil day, and having done all, to stand. Stand therefore, having girded your waist with truth, having put on the breastplate of righteousness, and having shod your feet with the preparation of the gospel of peace; above all, taking the shield of faith with which you will be able to quench all the fiery darts of the wicked one. And take the helmet of salvation, and the sword of the Spirit, which is the word of God; praying always with all prayer and supplication in the Spirit, being watchful to this end with all perseverance and supplication for all the saints and for me, that utterance may be given to me, that I may open

my mouth boldly to make known the mystery of the gospel, for which I am an ambassador in chains; that in it I may speak boldly, as I ought to speak.

—Ephesians 6:13-20

Girding our waist with truth is the divinely inspired *Word of God.* The breastplate of righteousness means "our personal righteousness is nothing but filthy rags" (Isaiah 64:9). Only as we stand in God's righteousness are we able to serve without having selfish motives. Having our feet shod with the preparation of the gospel of peace is the peace we experience in ourselves, within the community, and with God. We go forth as Jesus did seeking to save the lost. What we have is just not for us but is meant to be shared. The shield of faith is a huge shield we can hide behind so nothing can harm us. We entrust our physical and spiritual lives to God's care. The helmet of salvation is saving us from the penalty of our sins past, present, and future. Jesus' death on the cross gives us eternal life. The sword of the spirit is an offensive weapon. Empowered by God we take back everything our enemy (Satan) has stolen from us.

CONCLUSION

CONGRATULATIONS—YOU DID IT! All of your hard work and dedication has paid off. You are graduating *Bible Basic Training*. Enlisting in God's Army, you recognize the importance of developing a greater understanding of who God is, of Jesus' life of sacrifice, and his new expectations for you. At times life may seem difficult, particularly when you lose your way, not knowing where to go or what to do. That's why it is so important to keep your Bible close by at all times, and daily read it. Scripture is the owner's manual for humanity. Though it's often ignored, like any other road map it will guide you through the haze and confusion of battle or the tedious monotony of a long journey.

Life as a believer is to be more than mere survival. God empowers us to live it to the fullest. We walk into a new full life of peace, joy, and adventure that awaits us. Buckle in for the ride of a lifetime. The spiritual transformation process is a lifelong journey and it begins with what you have learned in *Bible Basic Training*.

The military takes volunteer civilians and turns them into soldiers. Since becoming a Christian is not contractual, we cannot be held liable for neglecting our training. Many times new believers are not even aware that spiritual training is necessary or available.

The intentional discipleship process enables new believers to mature as spiritual beings. The atypical idea, "Once you are saved you are in" is a grievous error the church has left unchecked. Christianity is not only about the moment of salvation; it is more than just getting our individual future access into paradise (heaven). It is imperative for all believers to receive spiritual training immediately upon conversion, or later if it has been previously overlooked. Let us leave behind us the days when we were once enemies with God, and become lifelong learners of God's ways. Though we will occasionally, unintentionally, or inadvertently make mistakes we now march to the beat of another drummer. We are more than conquerors through Christ who strengthens us.

Military and Christian training enables us to fully function in our new environment. Awareness of our duties, responsibilities, and entitlements gives us the means to contribute significantly to our organization. But we must pursue an active relationship with God reading, mediating, and communicating with him daily above all else. Our time with God is a refreshing and restoring mental, emotional, and spiritual shower. Our spiritual record is wiped clean "just as if" we have never sinned. Fellowship with other believers and service to our community help us to develop a new set of life skills. We will never obtain perfection but we are getting "cleaner" all the time. There are no accidents in the life of a Christian; God has a purpose for each of us. He can transform us into the full potential that he has destined for us.

Tough training exercises our spiritual muscles and prepares us for success in combat and life. Now that you've graduated, it's time for celebration. Get ready to transition to a new duty station with new knowledge and training. You will meet new people while continuing to build on what you have learned. Doing nothing with your training is pointless. Only as you continue on will you be able to achieve optimum performance when called upon.

Bible Basic Training is not meant to be a complete package; it lays a foundation on which to build upon. Relax in the knowledge that God is in control. Press on and do all God called you to do for his glory and honor. You do not have to be a licensed minister to make a difference. Get up, get active, and make a difference! You have the calling of God upon your life. Be a better parent, brother, sister, friend or co-worker. Reevaluate your time to add more God centered activities.

Live long and prosper in the Lord!

WinePressPublishing
Great Books, Defined.

To order additional copies of this book call:
1-877-421-READ (7323)
or please visit our website at
www.WinePressbooks.com

If you enjoyed this quality custom-published book,
drop by our website for more books and information.

www.winepresspublishing.com
"Your partner in custom publishing."